"*The Trusted Advisor* offers an invaluable road map to all those who seek to develop truly special relationships with their clients."

— *Carl Stern, CEO, Boston Consulting Group*

"This is a major contribution to the consulting profession, a richly illustrated and humanistic look at what differentiates a truly great advisor from a good one. This book will be valuable reading for the novice and experienced professional alike."

— *John Lynch, Chairman and CEO, Towers Perrin*

"Our company's development has been guided by and benefited from *The Trusted Advisor* concepts— and they work!"

— *George Colony, Chairman and CEO, Forrester Research*

"This book provides valuable insight into how one can become and, equally important, remain a trusted advisor, which is essential to success in a wide variety of professions."

— *Howard G. Paster, Chairman and CEO, Hill and Knowlton*

"This book is engaging, enjoyable and absolutely on target. It is packed with truth. *The Trusted Advisor* will guide success, not just in the advisory professions but in leadership and life as well."

— *William F. Stasior, Senior Chairman and Former CEO,*
Booz·Allen & Hamilton

"*The Trusted Advisor* will make any advisor more effective in winning and servicing clients' business. It is a must-read for anyone working in professional service firms."

— *Thomas W. Watson, Chief Growth Officer, Omnicom Group*

"*The Trusted Advisor* is right on the mark. Required reading for all professionals."

— *Hobson Brown, Jr., President and CEO, Russell Reynolds Associates*

"*The Trusted Advisor* will help advisors everywhere learn how to take their client relationships to a higher level."

— *Dale Gifford, Chief Executive, Hewitt Associates*

"*The Trusted Advisor* gets to the heart and soul of the advice business. This pathbreaking book is a must-read."

— *Professor Charles Fombrun, Leonard N. Stern School of Business,*
New York University

"*The Trusted Advisor* is a masterful work with valuable examples, constructs, and recommendations. The authors should be lauded for sharing their wealth of experience and advice on this critical topic."

— *David C. Munn, President and CEO,*
Information Technology Services Marketing Association

*f*P

The
TRUSTED
ADVISOR

DAVID H. MAISTER

CHARLES H. GREEN

ROBERT M. GALFORD

THE FREE PRESS

New York • London • Toronto • Sydney • Singapore

THE FREE PRESS

A Division of Simon & Schuster, Inc.
1230 Avenue of the Americas
New York, NY 10020

THE FREE PRESS and colophon are trademarks
of Simon & Schuster Inc.

Designed by Lisa Chovnick

Manufactured in the United States of America

10   9   8   7   6   5   4   3   2

Library of Congress Cataloging-in-Publication Data is available

ISBN 0-7432-0414-X

To Kathy,
Renée, Ashley, and Marshall,
Susan, Katy, and Luke

CONTENTS

INTRODUCTION

WE WROTE THIS BOOK because, in the course of our careers as consultants, and as advisors to other professionals (some fifty years of experience among the three of us), we have made every mistake we describe in the book and broken every piece of advice it contains. Whatever wisdom this book contains has been learned the hard way.

Our formal education served us well, but nothing in it prepared us for the real world of trying to serve clients effectively. Along the way, we learned that becoming a good advisor takes more than having good advice to offer. There are additional skills involved, ones that no one ever teaches you, that are critical to your success.

Most important, we learned that you don't get the chance to employ advisory skills until you can get someone to trust you enough to share their problems with you. No one ever taught us how to do that either. Yet we had to learn it. Somehow.

For many years, Rob Galford and Charlie Green have been conducting workshops, seminars, and training programs for some of the world's most prominent professional firms, under the title of "The Trusted Advisor." Meanwhile, David Maister was consulting and writing about professionalism, advice giving, client relationships, and other related topics. We met when we found ourselves presenting at the same conference and realized that, separately, we each had a piece of the puzzle. Together, we think we have a total picture to present.

The theme of this book is that the key to professional success is not just technical mastery of one's discipline (which is, of course, essential), but also the ability to work with clients in such a way as to earn their trust and gain their confidence.

We therefore address this book to both would-be advisors and to existing advisors who seek to create trust in their business relationships. We have written it mostly for *individuals* working in the advisory professions: consulting, accounting, law, engineering, public relations, executive search, insurance brokerage, investment banking, and similar activities. We have written it that way because that is the world we know.

However, we hope that professionals working inside corporations and other organizations, who also have clients and projects, will find this book relevant to their work.

Trust takes place between two individuals. It can, of course, take place inside organizations, within teams, and in other group settings, but we have chosen in this book to focus on the primary aspect of trust, that which occurs between two individuals, an advisor serving a client.

Ambitious professionals invest tremendous energy in improving business skills, including sharpening their specific expertise, gaining experience, broadening their knowledge, and "networking," all requiring hard work. However, seldom do they give enough thought to creating trust relationships with clients, and little guidance is provided by their firms on how to accomplish this. Many professionals do not know how to think about or examine trust relationships.

Unfortunately, there are many signs that trust is scarce. With ever-increasing frequency, clients conduct a microscopic examination of their professional provider's bills, challenging expenses, questioning how projects were staffed and how much time various tasks required. Clients often exclude lawyers, accountants, consultants, and other professionals from early stages of discussions because their conception of the professional's role is too narrow. Even long-term suppliers are forced to compete for new work through beauty contests and other proposal activities. Detailed reporting from professionals is often demanded so that the clients can monitor their activity.

What a change this represents! There was a time when clients trusted professionals automatically, based solely upon their honorable calling. Sound character and reputation were assumed, and business was conducted with confidence, bound by a handshake. Great firms and institutions were born and built on this natural expectation of trust.

Although that world may be gone, the need for trust has not disappeared. What has taken its place is the necessity to earn trust (and maintain it) throughout a professional's career.

Each of us has run numerous seminars and workshops with a wide variety of professionals on various aspects of dealing with clients. Among the most common questions we receive at these meetings are:

1. How can I get access to my clients more often?
2. How can I persuade my client to introduce me to others in their organization?
3. How can I cross-sell?
4. How can I avoid being typecast, labeled as a specialist only in my main discipline?
5. What do I do about not being an expert in related fields?
6. How do I get clients less focused on price?
7. How do I get clients to play fairly with me?

The answers to these questions (and many similar ones) have the same basis. You've got to earn your client's trust! Without that, none of these ambitions can be realized. All these questions require the client to either do something for you, or to decide to give you what you want. We believe that a client is most likely to give you what you want if he or she trusts you.

We believe that earning trust is an activity that can be managed and improved, without trivializing or mechanizing the advisory relationship.

In this book, we provide a new understanding of the importance and potential of trust relationships with clients, and show how trust can be employed to achieve a wide range of rewards. We examine trust as a process, which has beginnings and endings, which can be derailed and encouraged, and which takes place across time and experience. We analyze the key components of trust and the process by which trust evolves in a relationship.

We also explore the core capabilities that are exhibited by the trusted advisor, map the trust development process, and reveal the capabilities that must be developed to successfully navigate the process. We help you determine the level of trust in your current relationship and show you how to be more worthy of trust, and how to make that worthiness manifest to your clients.

HOW TO USE THIS BOOK

THE TERMS *trust* and *advisor* are seemingly small words, but they have meanings that have many layers and complexities. Accordingly, this book approaches our topic from a number of perspectives.

The book is like an hourglass: broad and diverse in Parts One and Three, focused and more tightly integrated in Part Two.

The chapters in Part One are full of anecdotes, practical suggestions, illustrations, and stories. They are designed to stimulate your thinking about a variety of interrelated issues, concepts, and skills that trusted advisors must consider.

The chapters in Part Two represent our attempt to bring structure to the topic, and are more formal in approach, if not in language.

Part Three contains chapters that build on Parts One and Two and apply the concepts and techniques introduced previously. The chapters in this section contain some new content as well.

You will quickly discover that we like to use lists. Not only do they convey information concisely, but they also (we hope) invite you to react and modify the lists based on your own thinking and ongoing experience.

For your convenience, we have duplicated all of the lists in the book in the Appendix. You might find it helpful to use it in any of three ways:

1. Begin your reading of this book by skimming the Appendix, which will give you a flavor of what the book contains and where it is going.

2. Use the collected lists therein to quickly identify a topic of particular interest to you and go directly to the relevant portion of the book.

3. Use it after you have finished reading the book as a quick ready reference (now and in the future), modifying the lists based on your own ongoing experience.

PERSPECTIVES ON TRUST

WE BEGIN WITH A BRIEF "sneak preview" of the book's themes, defining what we mean by the term *trusted advisor* and exploring the benefits that accrue to trusted advisors.

We then focus on three basic skills that a trusted advisor needs: (1) earning trust; (2) giving advice effectively; and (3) building relationships.

Next we discuss the mindsets or attitudes that are essential to becoming a trusted advisor. In closing, we explore the question of whether building trust is a matter of technique or sincerity (or both).

1

A Sneak Preview

Let's start with a question: What benefits would you obtain if your clients trusted you more?

Here's our list. The more your clients trust you, the more they will:

1. Reach for your advice
2. Be inclined to accept and act on your recommendations
3. Bring you in on more advanced, complex, strategic issues
4. Treat you as you wish to be treated
5. Respect you
6. Share more information that helps you to help them, and improves the quality of the service you provide
7. Pay your bills without question
8. Refer you to their friends and business acquaintances
9. Lower the level of stress in your interactions
10. Give you the benefit of the doubt
11. Forgive you when you make a mistake
12. Protect you when you need it (even from their own organization)
13. Warn you of dangers that you might avoid
14. Be comfortable and allow you to be comfortable
15. Involve you early on when their issues begin to form, rather than later in the process (or maybe even call you first!)
16. Trust your instincts and judgments (including those about other people such as your colleagues and theirs)

We would all like to have such professional relationships! This book is about what you must do to obtain these benefits.

What changes would *you* make to this list? What would you add? Delete?

Next, let's consider three additional questions:

Do *you* have a trusted advisor, someone you turn to regularly to advise you on all your most important business, career, and perhaps even personal decisions?

If you do, what are the characteristics of that person?

If you do not, what characteristics *would* you look for in selecting *your* trusted advisor?

Here is a listing of traits that our trusted advisors have in common. They:

1. Seem to understand us, effortlessly, and like us
2. Are consistent (we can depend on them)
3. Always help us see things from fresh perspectives
4. Don't try to force things on us
5. Help us think things through (it's our decision)
6. Don't substitute their judgment for ours
7. Don't panic or get overemotional (they stay calm)
8. Help us *think* and separate our logic from our emotion
9. Criticize and correct us gently, lovingly
10. Don't pull their punches (we can rely on them to tell us the truth)
11. Are in it for the long haul (the relationship is more important than the current issue)
12. Give us reasoning (to help us think), not just their conclusions
13. Give us options, increase our understanding of those options, give us their recommendation, and let us choose
14. Challenge our assumptions (help us uncover the false assumptions we've been working under)
15. Make us feel comfortable and casual personally (but they take the issues seriously)
16. Act like a real person, not someone in a role
17. Are reliably on our side and always seem to have our interests at heart

18. Remember everything we ever said (without notes)

19. Are always honorable (they don't gossip about others, and we trust their values)

20. Help us put our issues in context, often through the use of metaphors, stories, and anecdotes (few problems are completely unique)

21. Have a sense of humor to diffuse (our) tension in tough situations

22. Are smart (sometimes in ways we're not)

What would *you* add to (or delete from) this list?

Using the Golden Rule (we should treat others as we wish to be treated), we can probably make a fair assumption (or at least a good first approximation) that this list, or your list, is not much different from a list your clients would make.

So, if you want your clients to treat you as their trusted advisor, then you must meet as many of the "tests" on this list as possible.

Ask yourself: Which of these traits do my clients think I possess? (Not what *you* think you possess, but what *they* think you do!) If you suspect that you might not demonstrate all these traits, then how do you get better at each of them? That's what this book will try to answer.

Note that this book is not (just) about the wonderful benefits that wait at the end of the rainbow for the full-fledged trusted advisor, who does (or is) everything listed here. The early benefits of beginning to earn trust are substantial and can be obtained quickly. The ability to earn trust is a learnable skill, and we shall try in the succeeding pages to show "the yellow brick road" that leads to success.

2

What Is a Trusted Advisor?

NONE OF US BEGINS our career as a trusted advisor, but that is the status to which most of us aspire. We usually begin as vendors, performing a specific task or "one-off" service, employing our technical skills (see Figure 2-1). We may perform with excellence and expertise, but our activities are limited in scope.

At the next level, the client may sense that we possess capabilities not directly related to our original area of expertise. When operating at this level, we begin to focus on our ability to solve more general problems and not solely on our technical mastery. Our clients see us increasingly this way as well and begin to call upon us for issues with more breadth, and earlier on in the initial defining stages of their problems.

Fig. 2.1. The Evolution of a Client-Advisor Relationship

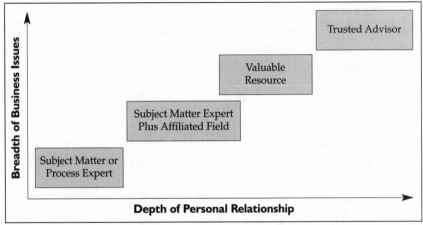

At the third level (valuable resource) we might be consulted on broad strategy issues related to our specific expertise, but not limited only to that expertise. We are no longer seen through the client's eyes as having just technical expertise or problem-solving ability, but we are seen in terms of our ability to put issues in context and to provide perspective. We begin to offer advice proactively and to identify issues in their organizational context.

The highest level, the pinnacle, is that of trusted advisor, in which virtually all issues, personal and professional, are open to discussion and exploration. The trusted advisor is the person the client turns to when an issue first arises, often in times of great urgency: a crisis, a change, a triumph, or a defeat.

Issues at this level are no longer seen merely as organizational problems, but also involve a personal dimension. Becoming a trusted advisor at the pinnacle level requires an integration of content expertise with organizational and interpersonal skills.

These levels, depicted in Figure 2-1, are a function of both "breadth of issues" and "depth of personal relationship." By "breadth of issues" we mean the range of business issues in which the advisor gets involved. By "depth of personal relationship," we mean the extent to which the client permits us to address their personal relationship to the issues at hand (and the business at large).

We do not suggest that a professional operating at Level 1 is doing something wrong. Far from it. Most of our daily professional lives are spent operating at Levels 1 and 2; relatively little of our time is spent actually working at Levels 3 and 4. The issue is not hours in a day, but rather the ability to shift comfortably and instantly to any level when necessary.

Another way of looking at the stages in the evolution of a client-advisor relationship is shown in Figure 2-2. It uses the same axes: breadth of business issues and depth of personal relationship.

Marketing people are fond of pointing out three kinds of professional-client relationships, which correspond to three approaches to winning business. These are product/service-based, needs-based, and relationship-based approaches. It is usually argued that the best, the most highly evolved of these three types is the relationship-based mode.

We think the distinctions are useful, but the conclusions are not quite right. As we suggested in Figure 2-1, there are times when it

Fig. 2.2. Four Types of Relationship

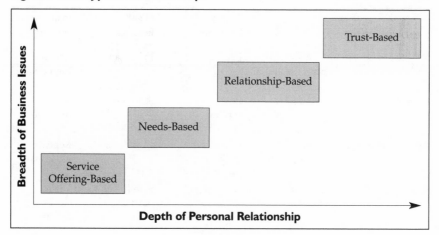

is perfectly appropriate and right for a relationship to be service based, or needs-based. And there are times when a particular type of relationship is *not* the appropriate one.

Most important, we feel a fourth type of relationship is missing from the typology, the trust-based relationship. The difference between this and the other levels is the human dimension, the recognition of the interpersonal, individual aspects of the relationship.

It can be seen that the full trust-based relationship is marked by a broad range of business issues and a deep personal relationship.

Figure 2-3 summarizes the characteristics of operating at the different levels shown in Figure 2-2. Each level has different implications for the focus, the time and energy spent, for what the client receives from the relationship, and for indicators of success.

Pinnacle Relationships

Extreme examples are often useful for highlighting key aspects of an issue. So it is with pinnacle relationships and trust.

One advisor who has reached the pinnacle of trust with his client is David Falk, agent to basketball superstar Michael Jordan.

Falk helped to create and to build Michael Jordan into one of the world's most successful "brands," starting with the 1977 Nike endorsement deal, then worth $2.5 million plus royalties. Eventually, Jordan endorsed dozens of products, from phone service to

Fig. 2.3. Characteristics of Relationship Levels

	Focus Is On:	Energy Spent on:	Client Receives:	Indicators of Success:
Service-based	Answers, expertise, input	Explaining	Information	Timely, high quality
Needs-based	Business problem	Problem-solving	Solutions	Problems resolved
Relationship-based	Client organization	Providing insights	Ideas	Repeat business
Trust-based	Client as individual	Understanding the client	Safe haven for hard issues	Varied; e.g. creative pricing

golf-club covers, and is worth many millions of dollars. Falk, too, has profited handsomely from this relationship. With Jordan as a client, he was able to develop an agency that eventually sold for $100 million.

Henry Louis Gates, Jr., writing in *The New Yorker*, recounted how Falk was "exquisitely attuned" to Jordan's attitudes about money and Falk's fees. In two instances, Falk reduced or waived specific fees (without being asked by Jordan) because he knew that's what Jordan wanted, even though Michael would never make such a request. Falk believes that this is one of the reasons the two are still working together, and that Falk continues to collect 4 percent of Jordan's enormous earnings.

The trusted advisor acts variously as a mirror, a sounding board, a confessor, a mentor, and even, at times, the jester or fool. The following excerpt from a conversation between Bill Gates and Warren Buffett is telling:

Gates: It's important to have someone who you totally trust, who is totally committed, who shares your vision, and yet who has a little
bit different set of skills and who also acts as something of a check
on you. Some of the ideas you run by him, you know he's going to
say, "Hey, wait a minute, have you thought about this and that?"
The benefit of sparking off somebody who's got that kind of brilliance is that it not only makes business more fun, but it really
leads to a lot of success.

Buffett: I've had a partner like that, Charlie Munger, for a lot of years, and it does for me exactly what Bill is talking about. You have to calibrate with Charlie, though, because Charlie says everything I do is dumb. If he says it's really dumb, I know it is, but if he just says it's dumb, I take that as an affirmative vote.

Richard Mahoney, former CEO of Monsanto, says of John Shutack, his trusted advisor from the management consulting firm Booz Allen & Hamilton:

"He irritated the hell out of me sometimes. But he wasn't a nuisance because he always gave good counsel."

How does it look from the advisor's side? James Kelly, formerly managing director and co-chairman of Gemini Consulting and now an independent writer and consultant, provides an informative glimpse of how a truly trusted advisor views the client:

"You must have a belief in the clients that you're working with. That's not to say that you accept them as being perfect. But there are ingredients in everybody that can and need to be appreciated at the same time that you may have to be working on the things that aren't so good.

"On some level all of us are flawed and inadequate; we have to accept that and do what we can to help with the things that maybe clients can't deal with in their particular setting as they might like to.

"So part of the role is putting your own credibility at stake on behalf of the client, despite the fact that he is (we all are) inevitably flawed. You support their strengths and help compensate for their weaknesses."

This ability to focus on the other person is evident in virtually all the trusted advisors we have encountered. We are not aware of any one approach that they have taken to get there. Some seem to have been born that way, with a blend of curiosity, equanimity, and quiet self-assurance that permits them to easily focus their attention on others. Listen to how James Kelly describes a client's decision to bring Kelly in:

"In his case it was a difficult thing to do because my client has such a strong personality. I've thought about it a lot, and I think it's because he sensed that I wasn't going to undermine him or compete with him in the same territory. In this case, I ended up having to coach him that he really was being counterproductive. But I feel it was almost like he knew that something had to be done, it's just that those messages had to be delivered by someone who cared. You have to accept and believe in the clients you serve."

In the deepest and most complete trusted advisor relationships, there are few boundaries within the relationship, little separation between professional and personal issues. Both members of the relationship fully know about each other and understand the role the other plays in his or her life.

Regina M. Pisa, chairman and managing partner of Goodwin, Procter & Hoar, L.L.P., one of Boston's largest and most prominent law firms, describes a most unusual and special trusted advisor relationship.

"I had a CEO client call me," she says. "He was leaving an appointment at Massachusetts General Hospital and wanted to come over right away. He walked in with his wife, and said that they had just been told that he was terminally ill, with not much time left. He said, 'I'm fearful for my wife. She doesn't have someone like you in her life who she can call on for anything and I want you to do for her what you did for me. We're putting ourselves in your hands to help us through all of this.'

"Getting the estate planning in order was the easy part. What they were asking for was for me to help them deal with the whole thing, before and after death. There's no greater definition of a trusted advisor, no greater reward than when you develop bonds with clients that run so deep."

This story stands as an object lesson for what can be achieved. Not all of us might choose to aim for relationships as deep as this one. But the story reveals that there are no limits to the depth to which a trusting relationship can go, other than those imposed by the advisor and the client.

Clients like Ms. Pisa's are the best clients because they understand the value of what you provide. In the push-pull of work, there are always deal pressures, missed deadlines, and so forth. Clients are not always understanding. They might be unreasonable in their expectations. But when you have relationships like this, clients treat you well.

Characteristics of Successful Trusted Advisors

Those professionals who apply trust most successfully are those who are at ease with concepts like:

- Do well by doing good
- What goes around comes around
- You get back what you put in
- Use it or lose it

These maxims are ways of suggesting that success comes to those who have chosen *not* to make success their primary goal. The way to be as rich as Bill Gates is to care more about writing code than about being rich. And the way to be a great advisor is to care about your client.

A common trait of all these trusted advisor relationships is that the advisor places a higher value on maintaining and preserving the relationship itself than on the outcomes of the current transaction, financial and otherwise. Often, the advisor will make a substantial investment in the client (without a guarantee of return) before the relationship does, in fact, generate any income, let alone any profit.

Based on the examples cited above, and the many trusted advisors we have encountered in our careers, we believe the following attributes describe trusted advisors:

1. Have a predilection to focus on the client, rather than themselves. They have:
   - enough self-confidence to listen without pre-judging
   - enough curiosity to inquire without supposing an answer
   - willingness to see the client as co-equal in a joint journey
   - enough ego strength to subordinate their own ego
2. Focus on the client as an individual, not as a person fulfilling a role

3. Believe that a continued focus on problem definition and resolution is more important than technical or content mastery

4. Show a strong "competitive" drive aimed not at competitors, but at constantly finding new ways to be of greater service to the client

5. Consistently focus on doing the next right thing, rather than on aiming for specific outcomes

6. Are motivated more by an internalized drive to do the right thing than by their own organization's rewards or dynamics

7. View methodologies, models, techniques, and business processes as means to an end. They are useful if they work, and are to be discarded if they don't; the test is effectiveness for *this* client.

8. Believe that success in client relationships is tied to the accumulation of quality experiences. As a result, they seek out (rather than avoid) client-contact experiences, and take personal risks with clients rather than avoid them.

9. Believe that both selling and serving are aspects of professionalism. Both are about proving to clients that you are dedicated to helping them with their issues.

10. Believe that there is a distinction between a business life and a private life, but that both lives are very personal (i.e., human). They recognize that refined skills in dealing with other people are critical in business and in personal life; the two worlds are often more alike than they are different, and for some, they overlap to an extraordinary extent.

The Benefits of Being a Trusted Advisor

To begin with the obvious commercial point, a trusted advisor benefits from having trusting relationships because they lead to repeat business from the same client. These relationships also lead to new business through referrals from existing clients.

These relationships are also less plagued by pro forma procedures that waste time and drive professionals crazy, such as proposals, presentations, studies, activity reports, and the like. In short, these relationships can be highly profitable, and more enjoyable, for the trusted advisor.

Another benefit is that in a trusting relationship, the advisor is able to employ the most prized individual skills and powers (listening, reasoning, problem solving, and imagining) and apply them to subjects that truly matter.

Time can be spent with a decision maker with substantial

power to affect an organization: create new initiatives, harness resources, and get things done. Trust frees us from the need to spend time on inconsequential projects or tedious procedural issues.

The world of media production provides an example of the efficiency benefits of trust relationships. Consider the stories of two (disguised) producers of television documentaries. Producer Thomas has, over the years, developed relationships of trust with a small number of television programmers (the executives in charge of developing and commissioning programs) and created a number of successful shows with and for them.

Now, to sell a new program, he simply creates a brief document (two to three pages) describing the basic idea. "There is no subject that an experienced executive has not received a proposal about," he says. "For the programmer, it's not about receiving a voluminous and costly proposal. It's about working with a producer they trust. If they like the idea, and need more information, they'll ask for it. If not, they'll simply give me the green light."

Producer Atkins, on the other hand, has a far less established reputation in television, and, following a less-than-successful relationship with one programmer, no strong trust relationship. As a result, he is forced to devote a great deal of time to producing weighty proposals that contain complete program treatments, biographies of the key team members, detailed budgets, and complex schedules, all elaborately produced with desktop publishing software, replete with graphics and images, and handsomely bound.

He exhausts himself (and his staff) in creating these proposals, only a fraction of which are, or can be, successful. As a result, he has produced fewer documentaries than Producer Thomas, and earns less money.

Finally, one of the most significant rewards of a trusted advisor relationship, for both client and advisor, is that in such a relationship, the individuals are most able to be fully who they are. The members of the relationship do not expend energy protecting themselves, and both can be open with information about their lives, their strengths, and their weaknesses. They share information and ideas, feel comfortable with themselves, and have great access to their emotions and inspirations.

Behaving with a professional colleague as you would with a friend (conducting yourself at the office as you would outside it) is an extremely valuable reward of a trusted advisor relationship. There is little pretense. Much work can be done without wasting time or words. There is no need for client or advisor to posture before each other. They are who they are (as imperfect as each of them may be) and do not allow their conflicts and incompatibilities to erode their mutual trust.

Getting Started

Few of us start with the skills of the expert trusted advisors described here. In fact, those individuals did not *begin* their careers with these skills fully developed. If we are to develop our trust-building skill, we must be honest with ourselves about how good at it we currently are. Many people assume they are better at winning trust than they really are.

A study was once done on pairs of graduate students and their faculty advisors. Each group, the students and the advisors, were asked a number of questions about themselves and their counterparts. The questions boiled down to the following:

1. How trustworthy have you been in your relations with the other person?
2. How trustworthy has the other person been in his or her relations with you?
3. How trustworthy do you think the other person thinks you have been?

The results were that each group perceived themselves to be more trustworthy than the other group. Not only that, they predicted that the self-perception of themselves as more trustworthy would be shared by the other person, which of course it was not.

If this study can be generalized (and we think it can), it reveals that we must work continuously to convince others that we truly are worthy of their trust. As a starting position, they think we are less trustworthy than we think of ourselves as being, and we have our doubts about their trustworthiness! There is work to be done!

We'll begin our investigation of how to get started by examining the three skills of earning trust, giving advice effectively, and building relationships. First, earning trust.

3

Earning Trust

To SEE HOW THE SUCCESS of your professional career depends on trust, consider your own purchases of professional services. Whether you are hiring someone to look after your legal affairs, your taxes, your child, or your car, the act of retaining a professional requires you to put your affairs in someone else's hands. You are forced into an act of faith, and you can only hope that they will deal with you appropriately.

You can research their background, check their technical skills, and attempt to examine their past performance. In spite of all this, when the final decision on whom to hire comes, you must ultimately decide to trust someone with your baby, which is never a comfortable thing to do.

When retaining a professional, what you (and your clients) want is someone who understands your interests and will not put their interests ahead of yours while working for you. You want someone you can trust to do the right thing. You want someone who will care. Getting hired (and getting rehired) is about earning and deserving that trust.

How to Win Trust

If trust is so important, how does one go about winning it? How do you get somebody to trust you? It is clear that it is not done by saying "Trust me!" Nothing is more likely to get the listener to put up his or her defenses!

The key point is that trust must be *earned* and *deserved.* You must

17

do something to give the other people the evidence on which they can base their decision on whether to trust you. You must be willing to *give* in order to *get*.

For example, David (Maister) once had to hire a lawyer to probate a relative's will. The first few lawyers he spoke with tried to win his business by telling him when their firm was founded, how many offices they had, and how much they would charge. None of this inspired much confidence. In fact, the more they talked about themselves and their firms, the less interested they appeared to be in David and his problems.

Finally, he encountered a lawyer who, in the initial phone call, asked how much David knew about probating a will. David's reply was "Nothing!" The lawyer then offered to fax to David a comprehensive outline of the steps involved, what he needed to do immediately, and what he should forget about for a while because it was not urgent. The fax also provided the phone numbers of all the governmental bodies David needed to notify, even though this had nothing to do with the legal work (or the lawyer's fees).

All of this (immensely helpful) information was provided freely (and for free) before the lawyer had been retained. Naturally, he got the business. He had built confidence by demonstrating that he knew what information was most relevant to David, even though some of it had nothing to with the practice of estate law. He had earned trust by being generous with his knowledge and proving that he was willing to earn the potential client's business.

Trust can be earned by the simplest of gestures. David has a dentist, named Andrew, who, early in the relationship, recommended that David permit him to perform various procedures on his teeth. Like many clients, David was not sure whether Andrew was recommending additional procedures because they were really needed or because he was just trying to increase his revenues (i.e., cross-selling).

David's view of Andrew was significantly affected by the fact that every time David (or his wife, Kathy) went to his office, Andrew *always* telephoned later that evening (without fail) to ask whether he (or she) was in pain, whether a prescription was needed, and so on. David and Kathy were very impressed by this. Andrew was acting as if he cared; unusual behavior for a dentist!

At first, David and Kathy were a little cynical. Did he care, or was he just acting "as if" he cared? Had he been to a dental marketing course, or read a client relations book? They didn't know. Over time, however, as Andrew's small gestures continued and accumulated, they came to believe that he was sincere. Today, they usually accept his recommendations for additional work. They have come to trust him.

Charlie and the Sandpaper

Soon after Charlie (Green) had been promoted to a managerial position in a consulting firm, he got a promising sales lead with a manufacturer of abrasives. His firm, like all consulting firms, valued those who could bring in new business, and he was eager to make his mark. He set up an appointment with the prospective client and invited a senior partner to join him on the call.

He and the partner were shown into the client's office, where they shook hands, accepted coffee, slid business cards across the conference table, all the while chatting and probing for points of connection and mutual interest: friends in common, shared experiences or backgrounds, similar attitudes toward life or business.

When they at last turned to the business at hand, the client focused his full attention on Charlie, and asked: "Now, what experience does your firm have in doing marketing studies for industrial consumables?"

In an instant, Charlie's mind seemed to have been sucked dry. He had no idea what was meant by *industrial consumables*. Then, a revelatory thought popped into his mind: the man is talking about *sandpaper!* But that knowledge only served to deepen Charlie's fear. He was sure that his firm had not done any such studies.

Charlie felt sure that if he told the client the truth, he could not win the business and would probably spend the rest of his career at his firm in leg irons and public shame. In the next millisecond, his training as a consultant kicked in, and he began formulating (in his mind) an answer.

"Not exactly," he planned to say, "but we have done many marketing studies, some of them for products quite similar to industrial consumables."

What products might be quite similar to industrial consumables, he would figure out later.

But, just as Charlie drew breath to speak, his senior partner leaned forward. He looked directly at the client, and said,

"None that I can think of."

He paused for a long moment. Then he looked the client in the eye, and continued:

"Given that, is there anything else that you think it would be helpful to discuss?"

The client looked unconcerned and then asked what similar experience the firm had that might be relevant. They proceeded with their pitch.

Had Charlie given *his* answer, it would have sacrificed his credibility and revealed his own focus on self-interest. It would have signaled to the client that he was willing to fudge his credentials. Who would trust such a person?

The answer the senior partner gave contained quite a different subtext. It said:

"I will answer your questions, directly and truthfully, even if it means losing a chance at your business."

In that moment, Charlie learned two important things about building trust. First, it has to do with keeping one's self-interest in check, and, second, trust can be won or lost very rapidly.

Charlie's firm won the business. He was not placed in leg irons. And he learned a lot about sandpaper.

A Lawyer's Moment of Truth

Peter Biagetti is a senior litigator at the prestigious Boston law firm of Mintz, Levin, Cohn, Ferris, Glovsky and Popeo.

A property developer who wished to sue his own mother, a partner in the family real estate business, had hired Biagetti to represent him. Biagetti got ready for the case, and a court date was set.

Just before the first hearing, Biagetti met the developer on the steps of the courthouse. The developer seemed to hesitate, his body language suggesting indecision, reluctance, and some kind of discomfort. Biagetti saw a man who was wrestling with a dozen issues that had to do with family pride, personal success, recognition, and filial love.

He knew that the lawsuit could resolve only one issue, and a relatively minor one at that. Drawing on the common background he shared with his client, he decided to comment on what he saw. "I told him that I found it hard to imagine how it must feel to go into litigation with his mother. I said I didn't think it was something many sons could go through with."

The developer might have upbraided his lawyer, told him to mind his own business, just do his job and get on with it. But he didn't. Instead, he stopped and looked at Biagetti. The developer decided not to press the lawsuit. Biagetti commented later: "I think he respected that we'd girded for battle, but were not so bellicose as to want to crush his mother. We settled the matter on the courthouse steps."

Soon after the settlement, the developer sent more work to Biagetti's firm, and eventually he decided to use Mintz, Levin for all of his business and family legal needs.

Another lawyer might not have sensed his client's underlying concerns, been blind to his courthouse hesitation, been unwilling to forgo the revenues of a potentially lucrative trial, or (most important of all) not felt enough affinity for him to speak up. But in this case, the client drew back a curtain and the lawyer was willing to look through the window. This is how a trusted advisor relationship often begins.

Not all of us will notice when an unusual opportunity has been revealed. Nor will we all have the quickness or confidence to respond to it. But if we have listened well, observed accurately, and spoken truthfully (and if there exists a degree of personal affinity), the client may welcome the expansion of the conversation. He (or she) may, in fact, take the opportunity to throw the window open yet wider still, revealing to the professional all manner of issues and concerns, aspirations and fears.

As in most things, however, timing is all. A successful advisor knows when to bother a client, and when not to. Alan Schwartz, of the Canadian law firm Fasken Martineau Dumoulin, notes:

"Clients are busy people and don't want to be interrupted with unimportant questions or barraged with requests for information or lengthy reports on matters that they consider to be an unwarranted intrusion on their time. Many years ago, a client called to report that they were very pleased with the lawyer that I had referred to them for a specific matter. His comment was, 'He knew exactly when to bother me and when to leave me alone.'"

Some Insights on Trust

How can we increase trust? Can we become more trustworthy?

To answer these questions, it helps to note some characteristics of trust. Specifically, it:

1. Grows, rather than just appears
2. Is both rational and emotional
3. Presumes a two-way relationship
4. Is intrinsically about perceived risk
5. Is different for the client than it is for the advisor
6. Is personal

Trust Grows

Trust rarely develops instantly, except in the face of a powerful experience. This may seem unremarkable until we note that other feelings develop much more quickly. We may say, immediately after meeting someone, that we like him (or that we don't). We draw similarly fast conclusions about whether we respect someone, or are bored by them. And we may very quickly say, "I *don't* trust him."

What we don't usually say quickly is, "I trust her." Instead, we may say "She seems like the kind of person I could come to trust," or "I might trust her," or "She seems to be trustworthy." Actual trust, as our language shows, is usually withheld, pending further evidence.

The fact is that trust does not happen without work, without volition, or without effort. It is not handed to us on a platter. Although we will later provide many suggestions, hot tips, and quick-impact actions, it must always be borne in mind that trust results from accumulated experiences, over time. There is no quick fix.

Trust Is both Rational and Emotional

Second, trust straddles the ground between the rational and the emotional. On the one hand, trust is based on direct experience of the expertise brought to bear on the client's problems. Content-free advisors are soon identified and rejected. On the other hand, as we saw in Chapter 1, we value trusted advisors for their support, their dedication to our interests, their courage in challenging us (with delicacy), and other emotional factors. As an exercise, go back to that chapter and divide the traits of trusted advisors listed there into rational categories and emotional categories. You may be surprised at what you find!

The significance of this for anyone in business who needs to deal with trusted relationships is profound. Much of business is transacted "as if" it were all in the rational realm. This is, perhaps, nowhere more true than in professional services. In our experience, there are many professionals who are *offended* at the thought that their relationships and their client effectiveness might be based on something other than pure technical competence.

Yet this is only half the story. While outstanding technical competence (or content) is a nonnegotiable, essential ingredient for success, it is not *sufficient*. Trust is a lot richer than logic alone, and it is a significant component of success.

Trust Is a Two-Way Relationship

Third, trust is a two-way relationship. One can love, or hate, or respect, or be fascinated by someone else, without the other person doing or thinking the same, or being in any way involved in the first person's activity. The same is not true for trust.

While there are things you can do to improve your trustworthiness, you do not have the ability to create a trusted advisor relationship on your own. Your client must participate and reciprocate. This means that you may have to select carefully those with whom you wish to build a trusted advisor relationship. No amount of interaction will add up to trust, if the efforts are all unilateral. You can't force trust.

The trusted advisor relationship takes place between two individuals and is highly personal. It involves emotion as well as intellect. It is dynamic and fluid. Building a trusted advisor relationship involves not only straightforward discussion, rigorous decision making, and conventional consultation, but also moments of revelation, late-night inspirations, odd actions of connection, and moments of epiphany.

Trust Entails Risk

Trust without risk is like cola without fizz; there isn't much point to it. If party A trusts that party B will do something, it means that party B (1) *could* do something different, (2) conceivably *might* do something different; but (3) because of the relationship, most likely *won't* do something different.

If party B couldn't and wouldn't do other than what party A expects, then the relationship would be just about probabilities and capabilities, not about trust.

The potential of trust violation is always there in a trusting relationship. The choice on the part of the advisor *not* to violate that trust is what makes the relationship special.

The levels of risk may, of course, vary from case to case. The risk of choosing the wrong attorney to assist a CEO in a multibillion dollar merger is very different from that same CEO's choice of a lawyer to prepare his or her will. The former is career threatening. However, while the latter may have less money at stake, it will usually still involve a perceived risk (and hence a need for trust) that is nontrivial.

When first encountering some of the trust-enhancing techniques we discuss in this book, many people are likely to say, "But that's risky."

They usually overstate the degree of risk, but at root they are correct. Creating trust entails taking some personal risks. It is the essence of trust. If you're not a little scared on occasion, then you're not taking a risk. And if you're not taking a risk, you're not likely to create trust.

Trust Is Different for the Client and the Advisor

Two people who love each other share the experience of love. One may love more or less than the other, and their degree of loving may vary from time to time, but the thing that they are doing (loving) is in essence the same.

This is not true for trust. In trust, one does the trusting, and one is trusted. The roles are not the same. Trust is more like ballroom dancing. One person must lead and one must follow, if it is going to work. If there is ambiguity about who is leading and who is following, then the dance collapses into (at best) two parallel exercises in solo movement.

This characteristic of trust has an interesting implication. Just because you can trust does not mean you can be trusted. However, if you are incapable of trusting, you probably can't be trusted. The ability to trust someone else is a necessary, though not a sufficient, condition for being trustworthy.

Trust Is Personal

Years ago, Texaco Oil ran a TV advertising campaign with a song whose lyrics went, "You can trust your car to the man who wears the star, the big, bright Texaco star." Perhaps times have become more cynical, but we doubt such a campaign would be aired today. And even then, the song said it was not the star we should trust, but the man wearing it.

The truth is, "institutional trust" is an oxymoron. We don't trust institutions, we don't trust processes, we trust people. We may come to believe that a given institution's behaviors are highly predictable, that most or all of its people can be depended upon to behave in certain ways. We may thus associate trusted people with a given institution. But we are still trusting a person and not giving blanket trust to a particular institution.

Trust requires being understood and having some capacity to act upon that understanding. Organizations per se are incapable of understanding; only their people can do so. Brand name recognition and reputation may get an institution on anyone's short list, but only a person can keep it there.

It follows that if trust plays a role for professional service firms, then it will find its voice not in advertising campaigns or in citations of experience or credentials, but in the human interactions between those firms' people and their clients.

In this sense, the movie *The Godfather* had it wrong when it said, "It ain't personal, it's business." The truth is, "It's business; it *is* personal."

At its core, trust is about relationships. I will trust you if I believe that you're in this for the long haul, that you're not just trying to maximize the short-term benefit to you in each of our interactions. Trust is about reciprocity: you help me and I'll help you. But I need to know that I can rely on you to do your part, and that our relationship is built upon shared values and principles.

If I am the client, then trusting you requires that I can believe you will do what you say you will do, that your actions will match your words.

And, perhaps most critical of all, I will trust you if you exhibit some form of caring, if you provide some evidence that *my* interests are as important to you as your own interests are.

4

How to Give Advice

HAVING EXAMINED THE FIRST of the three skills (earning trust, giving advice effectively, and building relationships), we now turn to the second skill: advice giving.

Many professionals approach the task of giving advice as if it were an objective, rational exercise based on their technical knowledge and expertise. But advice giving is almost never an exclusively logical process. Rather, it is almost always an emotional "duet," played between the advice giver and the client. If you can't learn to recognize, deal with, and respond to client emotions, you will never be an effective advisor.

Early in David's career, the management team of a large professional firm asked his opinion about how they were conducting their affairs. He responded with a very direct and candid answer. "Here are the things you are messing up, and this is what you should have been doing!" To his surprise, David was fired for being a disruptive influence. This was hard to understand, since he knew (and knew that *they* knew) that he was correct in his diagnosis and prescriptions.

Eventually, David learned the obvious lesson. It is not enough for a professional to be *right*: An advisor's job is to be *helpful*. David had to develop the skill of telling clients they were wrong in a way that they would thank him for giving helpful advice! He had to "earn the right" to be critical. Proving to someone that they are wrong may be intellectually satisfying, but it is not productive for either the client or the advisor.

Critiquing one's clients is, *by definition,* a part of every professional's job. Suggestions on how to improve *always* carry the implied critique that all is not being done well at the moment. Yet it is the person hiring you who is often responsible for the current state of affairs.

Lawyers are usually retained by the in-house general counsel; accountants by the chief financial officer; marketing, public relations, and communications consultants by the vice president of marketing; and actuaries by the head of human resources or the pension officer. More often than not, the person hiring you is a key player in the issues you are being asked to address. The advisor therefore needs to tread carefully!

Because of this, the diagnosis and solution of a client problem can never be performed without considering the sensitivities, emotions, and politics of the client situation. No matter how technical one's field or discipline, the act of giving advice is crucially dependent on a deep understanding of the personalities involved, and on the ability to adapt the advice-giving process to the specific individuals involved.

The Client's Perspective

To understand some of the emotions surrounding the client's use of professionals, think of the personal risks (reputation, promotion opportunities, bonuses, perhaps even one's career) that go along with the responsibility for choosing (and working with) any outside provider for a risky or expensive corporate matter. How would you like to be known as the person to blame if the corporate headquarters designed by the architect (that *you* chose) didn't work out? If the major lawsuit was lost? If the new marketing campaign failed to deliver the goods?

Viewed in this light, the client has every right to enter the process of using an outsider in a high state of anxiety. What's worse, the client's inevitable caution and trepidation are reinforced by the fact that outside professionals often see complications in a project the client doesn't see. In fact, it is an essential part of the professional's craft to reveal nuances, problems, barriers, and issues of which the client is unaware. If these are not conveyed with tact and skill, the client could easily believe (however unfairly) that, rather than relieving fears and being helpful, the professional is creating complications.

There are other emotional issues usually present as well. In the normal course of their business lives, client executives are people of accomplishment, authority, and respect within their organization. When hiring an advisor, they are forced to place their affairs for an uncertain period of time (and cost) into the hands of a practitioner of an impenetrable art, who often uses indecipherable jargon and engages in mysterious and unexplained (but probably expensive) activities. Predictably, the average client experiences unwelcome feelings of dependency or loss of control.

What clients frequently want is someone who will take away their worries and absorb all their hassles. Yet all too often, they encounter professionals who add to their worries and create extra headaches, forcing them to confront things they would prefer to ignore. ("Doctor, I came to you about my sore feet, and you are giving me grief about my weight. Can't you just treat my feet and leave me alone about my weight?") Since clients are often anxious and uncertain, they are, above all, looking for someone who will provide reassurance, calm their fears, and inspire confidence.

It can take some time for many advisors to realize that it is a central part of their profession to develop these interpersonal skills. Certainly no one ever teaches them to us in our training, either in school or inside the typical professional firm.

A Chat with Mom or Dad

Essential to being an effective advisor is having a good understanding of one's role. This is illustrated by a lawyer friend of ours, who once said:

> "Sometimes I feel like I'm explaining things to a child. My client can't seem to grasp even the basic logic of what I'm trying to convey. I feel like saying, 'Shut up. Just accept what I'm telling you! I'm the expert here!'"

What makes this lawyer's comments so understandable is that, in many advisory relationships, the client is untrained in the professional's specialty, while the professional may have seen the client's problem (or variants of it) many times before. There is thus an almost constant threat of coming across to the client as patronizing, pompous, and arrogant.

It is understandable why advisors can feel this way, and it is equally clear why clients resent it. After all, when I'm the client, I'm the one in charge. If I don't understand what you are saying, then maybe the problem is you, not me.

Maybe you don't know how to convey what you know and understand to a lay person. *Of course* I don't know your field; that's why I hired you! *Explain* it to me in language I can understand. Help me get it! Your job is not just to assert conclusions, but to help me *understand* why your recommended course of action makes sense. Give me reasons, not just instructions!

Although advising clients sometimes feels like explaining things to a child, the secret to becoming a good advisor is to do exactly the opposite.

We should act as if we are trying to advise our mother or father. If we are trying to convince Mom or Dad to do something, we are more likely to find the right words to convey our point so that it comes across with great respect, so that any implied critique is softened as much as possible.

This doesn't mean avoiding the issue, or rolling over and playing dead to whatever they say. It may be that what they are doing is disrupting the rest of the family, or is against their own interests. We *must* find a way to get our point across. Nevertheless, we must enter the encounter with the right attitude and with careful attention to phrasing.

When talking to a family member or a client, a primary task is to diffuse defensiveness (which, it should be noted, is *always* present). If we are to influence a parent or a client, we must find a way to prove we are trying to help, not to criticize.

It should be clear that we don't just tell Mom or Dad what to do (even if they ask us directly). Instead, we focus less on the advice (or conclusion) itself and more on creating a dialogue or conversation that helps them see the issue from a new perspective.

> "You've every right to do that, Dad, but Sister has a few extra burdens because of what's happening. Can you help ease the pressure on her? Is there anything we could do to help her?"

A business equivalent to this might be:

"That's a sensible decision. Before we settle on it, let's think through some of the implications. It's very likely that the dealers will be unhappy, and we need their cooperation in order to succeed. Is there some way to accommodate their needs so that we can keep them enthusiastically supporting the new plan?"

Finding the Right Words

Excellence in advice giving requires not only the right attitude, but also a careful attention to language. There are always a number of ways of expressing the same thought, each of which differs in how it is received by the listener. Saying "You've got to do X," even when correct, is very likely to evoke emotional resistance. No one likes to be told that they *must* do anything (even when they do).

It is usually better to say something like:

"Let's go through the options together. These are the ones I see. Can you think of anything else that we should consider? Now let's go through the pro's and con's of each course of action. Based on those pros and cons, action X seems the most likely to work, doesn't it? Or can you think of a better solution?"

If the client doesn't want to do X, the conversation is still alive. If you've said "You've got to do X" and the client says "No, I don't," you've nowhere to go. Your effectiveness as an advisor has just been lost, and you have placed yourself and the client on opposite sides. The odds are that what will follow will be an argument, not a discussion. (Naturally, the precise phrasing we have offered above is not the key point. You must find the words that work for you.)

Numerous other examples of "hard" and "soft" phrasing can be given. Take something as simple as, "What are your problems?" Seemingly a simple question, this can easily be taken as confrontational and challenging. A good substitute might be, "What is most in need of improvement?" As a quick rule of thumb, it is usually better to try to turn assertions into questions. Instead of saying, "This is the best solution," try the following: "My other clients usually do X for the following reasons. Do you think that reasoning applies here?"

Many years ago, when David taught mathematical statistics, he was at the front of the class, writing on the blackboard. Pausing from time to time, he asked the students, "Did everyone understand that?" There was silence in the room, and he therefore assumed he was doing just fine as a teacher. At examination time, however, everybody failed the test. He had failed as a teacher! He was frustrated because he thought he had created many opportunities to check for his clients' (or students') understanding.

A colleague pointed out that his attitude was fine, but his skills were weak. By asking, "Did everyone understand that?" he was creating an atmosphere in which students would have to confess weakness if they said no. His friend recommended that he change his question to "Have *I* made myself clear here?"

Phrased that way, it was easier for someone to say, "No, you haven't." Even if this was more challenging to David's ego, it gave him the chance to ensure that his points were being understood. Another way to deal with this situation would be to ask, "Would you like to stay on this point or move on to the next topic?" This is a neutral way of letting students (clients) express confusion about a topic (or lack of acceptance) without threatening their ego or embarrassing them. The principle here is that the successful advisor assumes responsibility for the proper mutual understanding.

All this shows that we aren't always aware of how we are coming across in our client conversations. We know what we intend to convey, but we do not always know how we are being received.

One device to help in this skill-building process is to rehearse a client conversation, with a friend or colleague playing the role of client. The simple act of watching another in conversation immediately reveals opportunities to spot those occasions where one could have phrased things differently to avoid the perception of being pompous, assertive, threatening, or unclear. And if we miss them, the other person can likely point them out.

If, in addition, you videotape the rehearsal, you get yet another opportunity for perspective. When we listen to others or see ourselves on video, the areas for improvement are usually blatantly clear. As the poet Robert Burns noted, there is no greater benefit than "to see ourselves as others see us."

A Teacher's Skills

In many ways, advisory skills are similar to those of great teaching. A teacher's task is to help a student get from point A (what they know, understand, and believe now) to point B (an advanced state of deeper understanding and knowledge). It is poor teaching for the professor to stand at the front of the class and say, "B is the right answer!" (As the old joke goes, a lecture is the fastest means known for getting ideas from the notes of the teacher into the notes of the student without passing through the minds of either.)

A teacher needs two skills to be really effective. First, the teacher must have a good understanding of point A: Where is the student (or client) starting from? What does he or she understand now? What do they believe and why do they believe it? For what messages are they ready? What are they doing now and why are they doing it that way? This understanding of one's student (or client) can only come from doing a lot of questioning and listening, saving one's reactions until later in the teaching (or advisory) process.

Having understood point A, the teacher cannot jump straight to a discussion of B, the end point. The second required skill is to develop a step-by-step reasoning process that takes the student/client on a journey of discovery. The goal here is to influence the student/client's understanding so that, eventually, the student/client says, "You know, on reflection, I think B is a better answer," to which the teacher/advisor can respond, "OK, that's what we'll do!"

This process is, of course, what is usually termed *Socratic teaching*. It is mostly accomplished through questions such as the following:

- Why do you think we have this problem?
- What options do we have for doing things differently?
- What advantages do you foresee for the different options?
- How do you think the relevant players would react if we did that?
- How do you suggest we deal with the following adverse consequences of such an action?
- Other people have encountered the following difficulties when they tried that. What can we do to prevent such things occurring?
- What benefits might come if we tried the following approach?

Socratic reasoning does take a great deal of patience. It is normal for the teacher to feel an almost overwhelming temptation to scream out, "But the answer is clear: we should do B! Listen to me!" This would be entirely intellectually correct as an answer, but a complete failure in advice giving.

Dealing with Client Politics

Among other things, effective advice giving requires an ability to suppress one's own ego and emotional needs. The most effective way to influence a client is to help the person feel that the solution was (to a large extent) his or her idea, or at the very least, his or her decision.

One way to do this is to help the client understand all the available options by conducting a thorough exploration of advantages, disadvantages, risks, and costs. You can then gently guide the client to the preferred solution. Notice that this usually means avoiding the temptation to take a stand too early in the process. An advisor's role is to be an expert guide in the process of reasoning through the problem. Our ability to be accepted as trustworthy guides can be damaged if our client believes we have already reached our own inflexible conclusion.

A good process for the advisor to follow is:

1. Give them their options
2. Give them an education about the options (including enough discussion for them to consider each option in depth)
3. Give them a recommendation
4. Let them choose

Some clients may want you to choose for them. But that, too, is their choice. If they ask you to choose, a tactful way to respond to this is to say, "If this were my business or my money, I would do X."

In extreme cases, your client might choose a path that you do not care to be associated with, and you may elect to withdraw. As painful as this might be, it is better than continuing to try to force your conclusion on the client. If your persuasive skills fail to work, and you can't live with what the client plans to do, then there is no other choice.

The advisor's role as a guide through the reasoning process becomes even more critical when dealing with committees, groups, or other situations where more than one person is involved in the decision. In such cases, one must learn how to assist one's client by surfacing and clarifying different points of view, and by building consensus among the client personnel. Rarely does an advisor have only one person as the client. Even if you are reporting to the CEO, it is usually the case that others must be "won over" in order for any action to take place.

Even powerful decision makers such as CEOs tend to involve their chief financial officer, their general counsel, or other corporate officers before a final decision is reached. Not surprisingly, since these people represent different constituencies, they each bring a different perspective to the problem you have been asked to help with. It follows that client politics are unavoidable in any advisory situation. If you can't deal with client politics, you cannot be an effective advisor.

Accordingly, all advisors must learn the skills and methodologies for bringing the different players "on board." For example, in many (if not most) advisory situations, clients schedule meetings involving a number of important players, each (usually) with his or her own agenda. Some advisors show up at these meetings and try to facilitate the session and deal with the different interests, agendas, and perspectives in "real time." Few advisors, however, are skilled enough, or fast enough on their feet, to deal with the many objections and concerns that surface during such meetings.

But if you are diligent about finding out who is going to be at the meeting, and disciplined enough to call each of them, one at a time, in advance, you can then ask each person to share their take on the issues, their concerns, and their objectives. Prepared in this way, it will be easier to plan and to run the subsequent meeting(s) and to help bring the group to consensus. Even though the individual agendas will not always be reconciled, it is likely that significantly more progress in decision making and buy-in will be made. While the up-front investment may seem insignificant, the return on this investment is usually substantial.

Most meetings also benefit from a quick summary of what was decided. People often leave the same meeting with different impressions of what was decided. Building trust also requires reducing ambiguities.

It is tempting (and probably true) to think that conflicting agendas, priorities, and goals are the clients' fault, not yours. However, unless you can develop the approaches and skills necessary to deal with these, your advice will not be acted upon, and you will not be seen as a helpful, useful advisor.

Customizing Your Approach

Giving advice is an art, not a science. Jeswald Salacuse (in *The Art of Advice*) rightly calls it a "performing art." Most of us have to learn these skills by trial and error as our career progresses. Individual tips and tactics are helpful, but to apply any of them unthinkingly across the board with all clients would be a huge mistake. The essence of advice giving is the ability to design a process and means of interacting that fits each unique client situation. We all have clients who have little tolerance for Socratic reasoning and who say, "Cut the nonsense; just tell me what you think." If that's what works with that client, then that's what we'll do. (We discuss different client types in Chapter 16.)

The burden, however, is still on the advisor to quickly understand each individual client's preferred style of interaction, and to be sufficiently flexible to deal with him or her in the manner that the client finds most comfortable and effective. The one thing the advisor must not do is commit to a single consultative style and say, "Well, that's my style. The clients can take it or leave it." That really would be pompous, patronizing, and arrogant!

5

The Rules of Romance:
Relationship Building

WE NOW TURN TO THE LAST of our three core skills of a trusted advisor: building relationships.

Sometimes our unconscious views of being a "professional" are based on distinguishing ourselves from our clients. In some ways, this separates us from our clients. But relationship building requires us to find common, not separate, ground. Thus the best metaphors for developing deep relationships with our clients are likely to be found in developing deep relationships with people from other aspects of our lives.

Business relationships have much in common with the relationships we try to build in our personal lives. For example, think of how you behave (or once behaved) in trying to build a relationship with your romantic partner.

To build a strong relationship, you try to be understanding, thoughtful, considerate, sensitive to feelings, and supportive. All of these adjectives apply equally well to what is needed to build a strong business relationship.

Fortunately, there are some key principles of relationship building that apply in both personal and professional life. Among these are the following:

1. Go first

2. Illustrate, don't tell.

3. Listen for what's different, not for what's familiar

4. Be sure your advice is being sought

5. Earn the right to offer advice

6. Keep asking

7. Say what you mean

8. When you need help, ask for it

9. Show an interest in the person

10. Use compliments, not flattery

11. Show appreciation

Go First

To earn a relationship, you must go first. You must give a favor to earn a favor. The one you are trying to influence must visibly perceive that you are willing to be the first to make an investment in the relationship in order to earn and deserve the relationship. Does this feel risky? It should, because it is. It is about taking the risk of rejection. In business it doesn't feel terribly different from the way it felt back in high school in the field of romance.

David's wife, Kathy, showed a profound understanding of this principle in the very early days of their courtship. David had told her that he was due to do some work in Egypt. She very much wanted to go along, but it was too early in the relationship to ask directly for such a big favor (a request that would have been received as pushing the relationship too far, too fast, too soon).

So, without referring to the trip, she casually offered to cook David a meal one evening. When he showed up for the date, he discovered that Kathy had cooked a complete Egyptian-style meal, served on a Middle-Eastern carpet. Egyptian music was playing, and there were a couple of tourist guides to Egypt on the table.

Now, how do you react to something like that? It was devastatingly irresistible. The message was unspoken but as loud and as clear as a bell:

"I'm willing to work to deserve your goodwill. And it's going to be fun to have a relationship with me!"

Naturally, they went on the trip together!

Illustrate, Don't Tell

To make anyone believe something about you, you must demonstrate, not assert. What you claim about yourself, your colleagues, or your firm will always be received skeptically, if it is listened to at all. Kathy didn't make promises and protestations about why David would enjoy taking her along. She showed him.

A similar example in business life is given by a professional firm, competing for some work from the Wells Fargo Bank, that arranged for its proposal to be delivered in leather saddlebags! They also had their proposal to Domino's Pizza delivered by one of their people dressed up as a Domino's delivery person. The professional firm was trying to send a clear message: "We are trying to treat you as special and unique."

Such tactics are neither "tacky" nor effective in themselves. They are frequently effective, but only if they are part of a pattern of gestures that reinforces the message! Isolated tactics will quickly be seen as insincere.

A primary goal of any relationship-building activity is to create opportunities to *demonstrate* that you have something to contribute. There's no better way to do this than to start contributing.

Some challenges: How do you successfully demonstrate (not just assert):

1. That you have listened to what the client has said?
2. That you appreciate the importance that the client assigns to what they have been saying?
3. That you understand the unique aspects of his/her situation?
4. That you understand his/her business?
5. That you are going to be a comfortable, supportive person to work with?
6. That you will be able to make a unique contribution?
7. That you can be trusted to keep your word?
8. That you have experience in dealing with his/her kind of problem?

We do not suggest (nor do we hope) that you have immediate answers to all of these questions (or that we have all of them). We do, however, have one piece of advice: Before you go into any meeting with a client (or prospective client), figure out the two or three things you want the client to absolutely believe about you by the end of the meeting.

Then, figure out, in advance, precisely how you are going to demonstrate that you *are* those things. Don't tell them, show them. Don't "wing" it. If the client is to be convinced of something, you need to be very prepared to *demonstrate* it convincingly. For example, your questions can reveal that you have done your homework:

"I know by the research we've done on your firm that you merged with ABC two years ago to become the third largest in the world. What I would like to learn more about is how you cope with the integration challenges of employees from so many cultures and backgrounds"

or,

"I read the speech you gave your trade association on this subject. I've reviewed your company's press releases. What I don't know is what kinds of options you're considering that may be too delicate for public consumption . . ."

Such questions give evidence that you are thorough, that you respect the client's time enough to be prepared, and that you are ready to get right to the issues.

Small gestures can count as much as big ones, as long as they don't become too rote. Take the issue of proving or demonstrating that you care about the relationship and value it. We will again use the parallel with romantic relationships. You get a certain amount of "credit" for remembering your romantic partner's birthday, your anniversary, and so on.

But consider the effect of showing up at home, on a random weekday of no particular significance, with a gift for your spouse. You hand it over and say: "There's no particular reason for this, but I was just thinking how much I love and appreciate you, and I wanted to make a small gesture of 'thank you' for all you do for me."

Now that's relationship building!

The business equivalent should also be obvious. On a random

day, of no particular significance, call your client and say, "I've been thinking about you and ran across some information I thought would interest you. I don't think it involves us, I just wanted to contribute the idea to you."

What are you demonstrating by this action? That you care, that you're thinking about the client in the client's terms, not yours, that you are a source of ideas (some good, some not so good), and that you are someone they will want to stay in touch with. Not a bad set of outcomes for such a simple action.

Listen for What's Different, Not for What's Familiar

At the core of earning someone's trust is convincing them that you are dealing with them as a human being, and not as a member of a group or class or subset. Accordingly, as you listen to a client talk, the question on your mind should be, "What makes this person different from any other client I've served? What does that mean for what I should say and how I should behave?"

Unfortunately, this is hard work. The natural tendency for most of us is to do the exact opposite: we listen for the things we recognize and have met before, so that we can draw upon past experience to use the words, approaches, and tools that we already know well. It's the way most of us work, but it doesn't always serve us well.

Before you can help someone, you need to understand what's on *their* mind. You must create situations where they will tell you more about their issues, concerns, and needs.

When you are on a date and want to impress the other person, you don't just think of "tricks" aimed at getting the other person to do or think something. (That's manipulation and is easily detectable and rejected.) Your goal is (or should be) to find out as much as you can about the interests, tastes, preferences, likes, and dislikes of this individual, to experience them on their own terms, not yours or anyone else's.

Only by finding out more about the individual can you decide if you want a relationship (is this a client *you* want?). Only by finding out more about them can you discover how to be more effective by understanding what will be truly appreciated and learn what this person responds to (i.e., how to get them to like you!).

One of the most dangerous sentences in any language is one that begins, "What clients want is. . . ." No matter how you finish that statement, you will be wrong. The whole point is that clients are, and want to be treated as, unique individuals. (The same is true in romance: there is no valid conclusion to the statement, "What women (men) want is. . . .")

Be Sure Your Advice is Being Sought

One of the biggest mistakes that advisors make is to think that their client always wants their advice. This is dangerously wrong. Again, the secrets of a great marriage are instructive here.

We know of a married couple, highly educated and both successful professionals, who cannot resist solving (or trying to solve) each other's problems. One will come home from the office, clearly troubled and under stress, and describe some problems at work. Immediately, the other partner switches into "solution" mode. "Well, what you should do is X, Y and Z," that person will say. The other will respond, "You don't understand. I can't do that because of A, B, and C." "Then do 1, 2, and 3" is the next comment.

Very quickly, the argument (and it *is* an argument) is getting very heated, emotions are rising, and resentments are building. While the advice giver is well intentioned (when presented with a problem, solve it!), the advice receiver is getting upset because he or she didn't *want* any advice!

What the advice receiver wanted was a combination of a sympathetic ear, emotional support, an understanding of the difficulties faced, and the opportunity to collect his or her own thoughts by talking them through in a nonthreatening environment.

This scenario applies without modification to business environments. All people, including clients, want affirmation, approval, support, and appreciation. In order to get your client to listen to and accept your advice, you must develop the skills and behavior patterns that ensure that you provide affirmation, support, approval, and appreciation along with your advice.

Like the overeager spouse, you must learn to hold back the temptation to say, early on, "I know how to solve your problem. You need to do the following." You may be right, but you will fail as a trusted advisor, and your advice will probably not be accepted.

Clients don't always want advice; they often just want a sympathetic ear.

Earn the Right to Offer Advice

In romance, there are rules of sequence. Certain stages of the relationship are not appropriate until other stages have been met and passed. Just as there are certain expectations that are unreasonable on a first date, but not after the fifth year, there are expectations in business that vary by stage of relationship.

The most common violation of this sequencing is the rush to give answers. We assume, frequently with complicity on the part of the client, that the client/advisor relationship is all about asking for and receiving technical expertise.

The truth is that receiving answers to important questions is not something anyone does lightly. We all want to hear solutions to our problems, but we are not at all inclined to take them seriously unless the person giving the answers has "earned the right" to give them.

Earning the right has three parts:

1. Understanding the client's situation
2. Understanding how the client feels about it
3. Convincing the client that we understand both of the previous two items

Keep Asking

The recommendation to "Ask a lot of questions, shut up, and listen" has been given often, but cannot be stressed enough. In business conversations, as in romantic conversations, people don't always say what they mean. When your spouse asks, "Would you like to have Chinese food tonight?" it is not necessarily a question. Just as frequently, it is a request ("Please, let's have Chinese food tonight"), or even an instruction ("Can we, for once, please, finally, have Chinese food instead of Italian all the time!"). Life would be easier if people always said precisely what they mean, but they don't: people hint a lot.

Similarly, there is some ambiguity in such client statements as,

"I'm not sure that will work." This could mean any of a hundred things, including:

- "I don't like the idea"
- "I like it but I don't think I can sell it to my colleagues"
- "It could work, but not in the form you've presented it"
- "I'm not convinced yet, but tell me more"
- "Drop the subject now or you're really going to start annoying me"

The skill of the trusted advisor is in framing the right (gentle) follow-up question that clarifies the ambiguity. How does the following sound, compared to a stark "Why not?"

"Yeah, I can see some ways in which that idea might not work here. Say more about it, would you, please? What, in particular, makes you uncomfortable with it?"

This should get the client to clarify his or her reactions, and give us guidance as to where to go next.

To your spouse, you might say:

"If you want Chinese, that will be fine by me. Personally, I never get tired of Italian, but if you want a change, let's go for it!"

Would that work? How would *you* say it? What are the words that work for you?

Say What You Mean

Of course, it is not only clients who are ambiguous and hint a lot. Advisors do, too. To be an effective advice giver, you must work at making sure that what you intended to say was actually heard that way.

The most common form of communication breakdown (and a major source of lost trust) is misunderstanding about what has been said. How many times in professional life has the following simple exchange taken place:

"You missed your deadline."
"It wasn't a deadline: I gave you an estimate of when I thought it could be ready."
"Well, that's not what I thought you said. Why didn't you say it that way in the beginning?"

Never assume the other person is a mind reader: Say what you want and think. Hints won't work. "The baby's crying again, dear." "Yes, how frustrating for you to have to get out of bed again. Good luck!"

If you need something from the other person, ask (politely). It's not enough to say, "I'm having a little difficulty with your staff getting me the information I need." (Hint, hint!) This stand-alone statement won't always get you what you want. ("Well, they're busy with other things; work around it.") You need to be clear and unequivocal:

> "Would you be willing to drop them a memo or talk to them about the importance of this? If we have to work around them, it will delay the work and add to the budget, and we really don't want that to happen, unless it's what you want us to do. How would you like us to proceed?"

Note that, with this language, the advisor is not just "rolling over and playing dead" to the client. Being a trusted advisor does *not* mean doing whatever the client wants: that's sycophancy. In fact, the truth is quite the opposite. Great trusted advisors can be relied upon to tell the client the bad news, along with the good. They can be relied upon to tell the truth, always with tact and care.

When You Need Help, Ask for It

Frequently, professionals feel they need to project an aura of complete mastery in order to win a client's trust. Nothing could be further from the truth. Anyone who tries to appear omnipotent, an individual with all the answers, is more likely to evoke precisely the opposite response ("Who is this guy trying to kid?").

Advice giving is, as we have noted, a duet, not a solo performance. It is more often the case than not that you will need to ask for your clients' help in solving problems. Don't be afraid to ask for it. You are more likely to be trusted if you say, "I'm not completely sure how to deal with this; can I talk it over with you?" than if you say, "Leave it to me; I'll solve everything!"

When you ask for help, you are keeping the focus on the client's problem or issue, and worrying a lot less about how you "appear." You are inviting the client to join you in joint problem solving: a sure path to building trust.

Of course, there are good and bad ways of asking for help.

In the hands of an expert, asking in subtle ways can be made to work very effectively. Another Kathy Maister story will illustrate the point. One evening, Kathy showed up in David's study at home and said, "Sweetie, I really have a problem and need your help!"

Naturally, David swung into macho, paternalistic mode: "Yes, dear, how can I help you solve your problem?" "Well," she said, "as you know, we are having friends tonight for dinner. I was just going over the list of things that needed to get done: shop for the ingredients, cook the meal, set the table, clean the house, buy the flowers, choose the music, and so on."

She continued: "I have made an estimate of how long it will take to do each of these things, and it looks like there is a possibility that I won't be able to get them all done perfectly by the time our friends arrive. And I do so much want everything to go well tonight. So, beloved, I was wondering if you had any advice for me?"

There's absolutely nowhere for David to go from there, other than to "volunteer" for something. What could have been an annoying demand ("Now, what I want you to do is . . .") was turned into a request for help.

The difference is not trivial. Demands are usually resented, while requests for help usually evoke a positive response. It is an interesting comment on the human condition that we often resent those who have done us a favor, and to whom we owe an obligation. In contrast, we feel kindly disposed to those we have helped. (This effect is described in Robert Cialdini's book *Influence*.) The syndrome is powerful and has interesting business implications. For example, trying to prove to a client how much you have done for him or her, especially when true, is as likely to breed a negative reaction as a positive one.

Show an Interest in the Person

There is no more certain way to make somebody think you are fascinating and enjoyable to be with than to keep them talking about themselves. This is not, or should not be, some phony ingratiating tactic (although it is often used that way).

Rather, it is a way of learning as much as possible about the person so that you can figure out the right way to say things so they will listen to you. If you want to influence someone, you must find out what influences them, or at least how they are likely to be influenced. The only way to do this is to ask questions, more questions, and even more questions.

When someone says "I think *this*," the appropriate response is not, "Well, I think *that*." Instead, you need to find out *why* they think what they do. So, you ask: "Why do you think that?" or "What led you to that conclusion?" or "Do you think it's always true, or just in certain circumstances?" The more they say in response to these questions, the better you will understand them, and the more you will able to find the right thing to say that will be both helpful *and* acceptable. An important part of trusting is having the feeling that "This person understands me!" These questions flow naturally if we have a genuine interest in the other person.

Not only must we ask questions, but we must also remember the answers. This sounds like trivial advice, but it is not. Some people can encounter someone they haven't met for months or years, and remember everything they ever said or did. Having seen this in action, we can report that it is incredibly powerful. People are amazed, because it is so uncommon. They have the reaction of "Wow! They must really have been interested in me!" There is a difference in being polite and being interested, and the difference is transparent to the observer.

Simple devices like taking notes and reviewing them before the next meeting can help a lot. (There is a lot of "contact software" around nowadays to facilitate this.) The goal here is not to fake an interest that is not real, but to use whatever tools you need to help you show that you really are paying attention.

Use Compliments, Not Flattery

Look for opportunities to pay a sincere compliment to the other person. Everyone likes and appreciates them, as long as they are rooted in truth.

The Italians have an expression for people who behave otherwise. They call them the *falsi cortesi* (or the fake courteous). Compliments must be specific enough to make clear that they are not mere puffery. "You look nice" has no credibility. "The color of that suit looks great on you" is better. Best is, "I believe you are an effective leader because I hear how people speak about you when you are not there, and I have also observed changes in the way your people do such and so."

Show Appreciation

Everyone wants to be appreciated. To state the same thought in reverse, there are few things more destructive to romance or trust than the feeling that you are being taken for granted. Naturally, this happens often, in marriage and in business.

Clients are rarely aware of the full scope of the "behind the scenes" expertise from which they benefit. They take it for granted.

Furthermore, while clients may rarely appreciate (openly) the efforts of the professionals who serve them, they do expect professionals to show their appreciation for having them as clients.

Imagine that you are a lawyer and are the client of an experienced accountant who has just found the means to minimize your tax obligation. You might think nothing of it, since that's what you hired the person for, and your appreciation might not extend beyond paying the accountant's bill.

However, if that same accountant should happen to retain your services to provide a defense in a malpractice suit, you would want to receive some degree of appreciation if you were victorious in your representation. So why, as the client, are we not appreciative of some professional's efforts on our behalf, when as the provider, we expect to receive significant applause?

The truth is we all want to be appreciated for what we have done. Not when we don't deserve it (that's phony), but when we truly deliver. Expressing (appropriate) appreciation to clients (and romantic partners) goes a long way in cementing a relationship!

6

The Importance of Mindsets

So far, we have examined three skills: earning trust, giving advice, and building relationships. Skills alone will not accomplish the task, however. In addition, a trusted advisor must develop appropriate attitudes or "mindsets." The most important of these are:

1. Ability to focus on the other person
2. Self-confidence
3. Ego strength
4. Curiosity
5. Inclusive professionalism

Focus on the Other Person

This attitude (or mindset) is summed up in the aphorism: "You'll have more fun and success by focusing on helping other people achieve their goals than you will by focusing on your own goals."

For some this sounds like an idealistic, spiritual, or religious principle. Others may think of it as communism: a cry to place others before yourself. A moment's reflection, however, will reveal that the aphorism is the very definition of what a capitalist exchange economy is about. To get what you want from someone, you must first focus on giving them what they want!

As Dale Carnegie said, "The only way to influence someone is to find out what they want, and show them how to get it." Notice that Carnegie did not say "the best way to influence" but "the only way"!

Tim's Story

Charlie once observed Tim White (then publisher of the *Albany Times Union*, later of the *San Francisco Examiner*) run an offsite meeting of his management team of a dozen people. Throughout this meeting, Tim conveyed a sense of technical mastery, calm, and wisdom. Yet he did so by hardly ever expressing an opinion, making a technical point, or articulating a decision. Instead, almost all of his input consisted of visually and verbally scanning the table, seeking emotional expressions on the faces of his team.

"Joe, you don't agree with that, do you?" he might say, or "Bob, you've got some pretty strong feelings about this one, don't you?" The meeting was highly successful. Not only were decisions made, but everyone felt involved and consulted and that the process was "fair."

Tim did not lack for technical competence, and he had strong opinions, but he achieved most of his ends by devoting his attention almost entirely to observing, understanding, and articulating the needs of others. He achieved high-content results almost entirely through low-content leadership.

It is this ability to stay focused on other people, in the face of a swirling set of demanding distractions, that is so problematic for many of us. Success at being other-focused is not a function of formal business tools but of personal psychology.

Impediments to Being Client-Focused

The prime obstacle to focusing successfully on the other person (in our experience) is the apparently common belief that mastery of technical content is sufficient to serve clients well. It is ironic that a business in which the serving of clients depends so heavily on interpersonal psychology should be peopled with those who believe in the *exclusive* power of technical mastery.

And yet, as David Nadler, CEO of Delta Consulting, puts it:

"The truth is, you can fix the content thing better than you can fix the collaborative thing. For some people with process consulting backgrounds, content can be tough. But in general you can train for content better than you can for collaboration."

Another major obstacle is the inability to focus concentrated attention on the client. In the midst of a conversation with a client, we are likely to find ourselves with thoughts like, "How will I solve this problem?" "How will I get the client to buy this idea?" "What am I going to say when the client finishes talking?" "How can I appear expert?"

If we are honest and strip down all these distractions to the core, we are likely to find some form of fear at the root. It may be fear of embarrassment, of failure, of appearing ignorant or incompetent, or fear of loss of reputation or security.

Ironically, the professions attract people who are prone to these fears. More often than not, we professionals are high achievers who have consistently overcome our fears through constant application of skill and hard work in the pursuit of technical mastery. And, up to a point, these things are rewarded. In the early levels of professional life, we are often asked to focus on little else.

Then comes that crucial career transition, from technician to full professional, from content expert to advisor. As technicians, our task is to provide information, analyses, research, content, and even recommendations. All of these are basically tasks performed out of the client's presence. In contrast, our task as advisors is an "in-person," "in-contact" challenge to help the client see things anew or to make a decision. This requires a complete change of skills and mindsets.

It can be unsettling to find that the client is primarily interested in having his or her problem understood, in all its emotional and political complexity, as a precondition to having the problem diagnosed and solved.

Some of us never make it through this hurdle. The key to prior career success (technical excellence) can actually become an impediment at this level. Then, the fears, which drove us to excellence in the first place, reemerge.

The kinds of people who typically succeed in professional service firms are often driven, rational, and meritocratic, with a great need to achieve. It is the natural thing for such people to stay focused on their own individual performance (something that is reinforced by many firm cultures), and to look for confirmation that what *they* are doing is all right. This is not a situation conducive to building skills in developing trust. It is in some sense a wonder that so many do so well.

Listen to what Stephanie Wethered, an Episcopal priest, has to say:

> "The key is empathetic listening. It's vital in the pastoral world. It involves the willingness to go to where the other person is, which is usually a very painful place. And you have to be in touch with your own pain to go there. If you don't know that pain, that terrain, you will not go there. It's about moving from 'I' to 'We.'"

Empathetic listening is a critical skill. And our ability to do it well, according to Stephanie, is in direct relation to how closely we can truly feel what the other person feels. Our ability to do that is in direct relation to how well we can leave behind our own self-orientation and our desire for self-promotion.

Charlie was reminded of this recently. He had started with a new client, referred in by another consultant. Charlie had fun preparing for the first conference call with the CEO, but he also spent some significant time wondering and worrying about how he was going to come across to the CEO.

As Charlie discussed the call later with the consultant who had referred him in, she said that she had spoken with the CEO and that he had asked, "Does Charlie like the project? Did he like me?" It was a reminder that, to a great extent, we all are overfocused on ourselves. Charlie's orientation was to himself; the client's was, too.

Learning to focus on the other isn't an instantaneous decision: it's a lifelong learning experience!

Self-Confidence

Insecurity (the opposite of self-confidence) is a common source of trust problems. We have already noted the common temptation, in a client conversation, of jumping too soon to "the answer." It is only human for the client to want to be understood before being ready to listen to advice. We *know* that, but it takes self-confidence to wait and believe that after listening and brainstorming, we will still have ample time and talent to discover the technical answer.

We are not talking about monumental levels of self-confidence here. It is sufficient to simply be able to focus our finite attention on listening and understanding, without believing we must squander it all immediately on problem solving.

Ego Strength

Ego strength is not the same as self-confidence. It is the ability to focus on the consultative relationship process, rather than on credit or blame attached to the search. There is an old saying, "It is amazing what you can achieve if you are not wedded to who gets the credit."

The flip side of credit is blame. A tendency to blame others, or circumstances, is generally a recipe for unhappiness in life. It is even more surely and quickly a recipe for failure in becoming a trusted advisor. Clients (and professional firms) place a great deal of value on those who take on great amounts of personal responsibility.

However, taking responsibility can become dysfunctional as well. Charlie once retained a psychologist to administer and interpret tests of successful and unsuccessful consultants. The results served mainly to distinguish each group from the population at large, by the huge amount of "responsibility taking" evidenced by the consultants. She explained: "These are people who would feel personally responsible for the weather if it rained on the corporate picnic."

At this level, what would appear to be the opposite of blaming becomes clear for what it is: merely another form of self-orientation. Just as wanting all the credit and none of the blame is self-focused, so is taking *all* the responsibility. Neither is client-focused.

Joe Sherman, the managing director of San Francisco's Fidelity Partners, describes what ego strength in an advisor meant for him.

"I had a huge ethical disagreement with someone, which had come to a head. I had brought along (my advisor) and he was listening to the tirades of this other person, and he was able to just listen. I was so emotionally attached that I couldn't let go. I could barely contain my anger. But (my advisor) was calm and direct, and didn't engage in the venom. He was able to steer the discussion to where it needed to go. Since then, that advisor has handled all my business and personal matters."

Ego strength allows one to focus on the matter at hand, and not on who gets blame or credit for getting there.

Curiosity

The right to solve problems is earned by informed listening, which in turn is driven by curiosity.

The key is to focus not on what we know, but on what we don't know. And that is curiosity: the constant asking of questions. "What's behind that?" "Why is this the case?" "How does this fit in?"

As curiosity does its work, problem definitions evolve. Patterns emerge, connections are made, and positions soften and re-form. Perspectives migrate, and richness of insight is gained. The "right answer" is never as right at the outset as it is after it has evolved, informed by inquiry. Curiosity is the attitude that drives the opportunity to contribute.

Inclusive Professionalism

Many professionals view professionalism as something that sets them apart from the client. There are "business people" and then there are "professionals." There are "corporations," and then there are "professional firms." Many professional firms work hard to create the sense that professionals, or the professions, are in some way separate, different, or apart. We think this is incorrect, dangerous, and self-defeating. The essence of professionalism lies not in distinguishing ourselves from our clients, but in aligning with them to improve their situations.

The attitude of exclusive professionalism (which restricts the label of professionalism to the advisor) manifests itself in a number of dysfunctional ways. It reinforces a misleading belief that the advisor's job is to solve problems rather than to help the client solve problems. It reinforces a belief that advisors must "control" or "manage" client interactions and relationships, as opposed to inhabiting them jointly.

Inclusive professionalism means acknowledging and engaging the professionalism of others. It means that the unique talents of each party should be brought to bear jointly for the greater good. It means joint responsibility for the effectiveness of work.

Whatever the reason, many of us in the professions are not very good at teamwork. Many of us collaborate very poorly, even with each other. Small wonder, then, that we don't always collaborate well with clients.

Most firms *say* they support inclusive professionalism, but we have found that conclusion, in many cases, to be somewhat self-deluding. We know consulting firms whose policy it is to not leave behind written materials, for fear that the consulting firm might "lose control." We know law firms that have strict policies on what "work product" clients may see, outlining an essentially adversarial relationship from the start. All these practices are largely based on an "us versus them" concept, rather than the "us" implied by inclusive professionalism.

7

Sincerity or Technique?

IN PRECEDING CHAPTERS we have offered advice on actions and words that serve to build trust (and relationships). However, we often get questions and comments from participants in our programs about the issue of sincerity. Is building trust about the use of the correct tactics, or do you have to like your clients, be interested in them or care about them, to make the tactics effective?

Even more challenging is the question: Is it appropriate to use techniques if you don't truly care? Is it possible to "manipulate" the emotions of another person without being manipulative? We think so.

An example may illustrate the point.

A friend of ours, Jim, is a self-made man, having bought and turned around a company single-handedly. He "gives back" in many ways, one being the teaching of a course at a local business school. At the first meeting of each semester, he brings a Polaroid camera and a white sheet for background, and he photographs each person. Then he tells them that he will memorize their faces, their names, their undergraduate schools, *and* their companies by the next class.

He then works very hard for the next week to deliver on his promise to a class of forty-five students. And, he stresses, he is not a natural at names and faces. He runs through the pictures and data, using flash cards to memorize the information.

For the next class, everyone shows up to see if he can do it. He does. He dazzles. And everyone stays throughout the semester. His no-show and dropout rates are zero.

Is what Jim does premeditated? Absolutely. Is it sincere or is it manipulative? We would argue that those are needlessly loaded words. Yes, he is consciously using a technique, visible even to his "clients." Yet it is equally clear that he is sincere, that he cares. Why else would a busy person teach a course for a small amount of money that he doesn't need, and devote hours of his valuable personal time to memorizing people's names?

Our advice is simple. If you already care about a client, then practice the behaviors that exhibit caring. If, on the other hand, you're only going through the motions, then you will be found out and will fail.

So, does that mean that if you do not actually care for the client, you should not adopt the tactics, techniques, and advice we recommend? No, that's not our advice, either. Remember Rodgers and Hammerstein's song "Whistle a Happy Tune?" It points out that "when I fool the people, I find, I fool myself as well!"

There is an old debate about whether you get people to change their actions by changing their attitudes, or change their attitudes by getting them to first change their actions. Naturally, it *can* work both ways. But it is often easier to first change one's actions (adopt caring behaviors) as a way to achieve caring than it is to change one's mental state (which takes more time).

Sincerity, the way we usually mean it, has to do with intentions; we assume it comes from within. But our clients have no way to observe sincerity except through external behaviors. From certain behaviors (attention paid, interest shown, advance work done, empathetic listening), we infer the internal state we call sincerity.

Thus, to ask whether we must care first or try out the actions first amounts to asking whether we should start from within, or without. The only right answer is yes to both.

By starting with caring (working from the inside out), we open ourselves to possibilities and become willing to go where the client will take us. The skill or action behaviors can then fall on fertile ground.

By starting with new external behaviors or skills, we open ourselves to new information and stimuli that encourage our thinking and allow for a fresh focus on the client. We do this when we generate shared enthusiasm for questions, eagerly exploring together the next implication.

Sometimes it's true that "you can act your way into right thinking better than you can think your way into right acting," or "you fake it till you make it." And sometimes the reverse is true. We are generally better off working from both ends to the middle.

Sincerity *is* crucial to both trust and relationships. If you have it and can show it, you'll do well. If you try to "fake it" (i.e., use the tactics without really caring), but *always* act that way, you'll probably end up creating something that is indistinguishable from the genuine article, either to the client or to yourself.

What will not work is the use of *occasional* tactics that are inconsistent with the way you *normally* behave. These will soon be spotted for what they are: phony, insincere, and clumsy efforts, and they will not only be ineffective but will also create an adverse reaction. There's no point to faking it, unless you plan to keep it up for the rest of your relationship. And if you always *do* keep it up, always exhibiting sincere caring behaviors, the distinction will become academic. As Gerald Weinberg said in his book *The Secrets of Consulting*, "The trick of earning trust is to avoid all tricks."

What If You Don't Care for Them?

We are not so idealistic as to believe that we can all care for everybody we encounter. Sometimes, even after trying very hard and applying every idea in this book (and more besides), you may find that you just can't empathize with this client. What do you do then?

Consider the options:

1. Keep serving the client, but don't make the effort to build the relationship
2. Keep serving the client, but apply the trust techniques without sincerity
3. Pass the client on to a colleague
4. Resign the account.

Not an attractive set of options, is it?

In Option 1 (serve the client, but don't try to get close), you will not only miss all the benefits of being trusted, but you will have a less than fulfilling work life. Our slogan is: "Life is too short to work with idiots; and that's just as true when it's our clients' lives and we're the idiots!" A lack of chemistry between you and the client may be as much (if not more) your fault as it is the client's.

Regardless of blame, if there is no chemistry there, then it only makes sense to either create the chemistry (somehow!) or move on. Our view is that Option 1 makes everyone a loser, advisor and client, and should be dropped from consideration.

Option 2, keep serving and try to fake it, is clearly worth trying for a while, as we have argued above. If you try hard to find the connections and empathy between you and a client, you often can. But not always! So, should you keep faking it? Not in our view. We can imagine nothing worse than to spend our whole lives faking it. If you've *really* tried to build a relationship and it's not working, move on to Option 3.

Option 3 is attractive when it is possible: Few clients are completely unlovable, and personal chemistry is exactly that. Someone you cannot connect with may be a dream client for a colleague. Consider this seriously.

Option 4 (resign) is the ultimate step, but there are occasions when it must be taken. If you can't bring yourself to act as a caring, trusted advisor, you *will* be less effective, perhaps even ineffective. You may think that financial pressures force to keep serving such clients, but this is a very short-term view. You do yourself no good by continuing to serve clients who can see that you are not fully engaged. The damage to your reputation will outlast any cash penalty you pay while searching for a client you can enthusiastically serve. Reputation before revenue!

That's all very well and good, you may be thinking, if you happen to be a sole practitioner or the senior person on the engagement. But what if you're a junior professional or part of a large team? What if you don't feel you have the luxury of resigning the account, or even passing the client on to a colleague?

We have three pieces of advice for someone in such a situation. First, check your motives. Are you sure you've tried everything you know to find ways to relate to this client? Are you sure you're not looking for a reason to avoid some other aspect of unpleasantness in the assignment? Are you sure the client would or has expressed equal levels of concern?

Second, put the issue in perspective. If it's not life-threatening, career-threatening or client-threatening, then how long must you live with the situation? If it's a matter of only a few months, it may not be worth the energy required to resolve it.

Third, if the issue is real and material, we advise you to raise it directly with the senior engagement manager. That person has as much at stake as you do. If they convince you that you are wrong, you gain peace of mind. If you convince them you are right, they improve their odds of providing good client service.

If you both remain unconvinced by what the other has to say, then you may have also learned something about your ability to connect with yet another person in your work life. This does happen, once in a while. At the same time, remember the sage person's advice: "I was amazed at how many fools I ran into until I noticed the common denominator in all those interactions: me."

Why do we in the professions so often avoid this whole topic? In David's book *True Professionalism,* he reported that a common survey result is that the typical professional really likes his or her clients only about 20 percent to 30 percent of the time! The rest are mostly "tolerated."

The professions include many people who are hugely talented intellectually, but some have paid less attention in their lives to social skills, and even less to emotional skills. Such people have a very difficult time accepting things that look, to them, like failure. The thought of a client saying, "This isn't working" is essentially indistinguishable to them from a client saying, "I dislike you and look down upon you as a person." What to others might appear a simple social fact is experienced as a highly personal criticism.

The truth is there are very few people who have the capacity to relate to everyone. It follows that there are going to be cases where "the glue doesn't stick." Ask yourself what percentage of people you have met in the business world really grab you, excite you, or make you want to work with them? Then ask what percentage of people in the business world make you want to resign your career, rather than have to spend any more time with them? And the (presumably large) middle category of people probably determines how excited you are about your profession overall.

Assuming you're like the rest of us, then at a minimum the same *percentage* of people whom you dislike will dislike you. And, from the broad middle category, there will be varying degrees of indifference about the prospect of working with you.

Worse yet, the people you dislike are not necessarily the same ones who dislike you. Just because you like someone does not mean they return the feeling. Even if the percentage of "non-likes" is the same between professionals and clients, the total number of fits will be less. No wonder we have cases of non-fit! Some nontrivial percentage of potential relationships just will not work.

A good rule to remember is that, in relationships, there are no win-lose or lose-win combinations: There are only win-wins and lose-loses. If the fit is not there for one party, then, just as for couples who ultimately divorce, it will, in the end, not work for either of them. To speak the truth about the disparity may be difficult, but it is usually the most efficient way out, not to mention the kindest.

Client or Friend?

Does all of this mean you have to make every client your friend? Not at all. You can be interested in someone without being their friend. You can deal with them as individual human beings, and avoid treating them as people in a role, without pretending that they are your bosom buddy. Clients quickly see through these false friendships, often built on extended conversations about golf, football, and similar topics.

Many professionals worry that it may be "unprofessional" to get that close to a client. We don't agree. Showing interest in the person does not mean intruding into private areas. We think it is unprofessional *not* to show an interest in your client. To convince someone that they should view you as their trusted advisor, you must first convince them that you are committed to them. McDonald's likes to describe professionals that serve them (such as advertising agencies) as having "ketchup in their veins."

Does this mean that you actually have to care? Yes, you do actually have to care, if you want to be a trusted advisor. If you want to be merely a vendor, you don't.

Rob developed a great relationship with Arnold, a director of a major firm. This hadn't been easy, as Arnold was pretty demanding, intellectually and otherwise. When Arnold left the company, Rob found that it was much more difficult to be as committed to the company relationship as he once was.

Rob tried really hard, certainly liked the people who replaced Arnold, and continued to do good work with and for them. He was given more work to do, but his heart really wasn't in it in the same way. He thought he behaved as he always had, but the strength of the relationship gradually diminished. Without true feeling, tactics will lose their power. Even when applied by someone who teaches this stuff!

Should you socialize with your clients? Occasional socializing can be enjoyable, but earning trust is not about golf games, dinners, and opera performances. While socializing is not necessary, being sociable is. It's the window into the clients' selves as people, their needs, hopes, and fears.

It's the Journey, Not the Destination

Most of us have very keen instincts about what our romantic partners are looking for in us. If they are driven by a genuine liking for us, we see it exhibited in a thousand ways, from being willing to pursue common interests to looking us in the eye.

On the other hand, if our romantic interest's objectives are aimed solely at something else (prestige, sex, money, comfort) we react negatively, and strongly so. The tension generated in relationships by unaligned interests is huge.

So it is in business. When we are buying something, we have very little difficulty in detecting whether or not someone has our interests at heart. Most people are too caught up in their own concerns to genuinely exhibit care for another's needs.

However, on those rare occasions when salespeople actually transcend their own concerns and are attentive to customer needs, the effectiveness of the sales process is dramatically enhanced.

One of the most important lessons to learn is that to earn trust, you must bet on the long-term benefit of the relationship. No relationship is without its rough spots; all relationships are cyclical.

The hallmark of trusted advisors is that they don't bail out when times get tough.

We don't want people to be interested in us as a means to an end, as a destination for their own purposes. We want people to be interested in us as fellow-voyagers, people who care about us enough to go on a journey with us.

PART TWO

THE STRUCTURE OF TRUST-BUILDING

IN THIS PART, we will take a slightly more formal approach and try to bring some structure to the complexities of earning and maintaining trust.

In the first chapter, we offer a simple but, we hope, evocative vehicle for understanding how different trust factors interrelate. This is followed by a five-stage trust development process, which provides a framework for us to explore the evolution of trust as the client-advisor relationship evolves. One chapter presents the process, and the remainder of the section is devoted to exploring each of the stages.

8

The Trust Equation

In this chapter, we offer a formula that will show how different trust elements interrelate. Naturally, the equation should be treated as a framework for looking at the topic, and not as a scientific conclusion.

We suggest that there are four primary components of trustworthiness, shown in Figure 8-1. The four components have to do with the trustworthiness of words, actions, emotions, and motives, as shown in Figure 8-2.

We can use the trust equation to isolate the impact of each particular component of the equation. Figure 8-3 shows the kinds of relationship failures that result from the absence of each component, one by one.

Most professionals, when asked to talk about trust, instinctively focus on credibility and reliability. "My client knows I am credible and reliable," they say. "So why doesn't my client trust me?"

Fig. 8.1. The Trust Equation

$$T = \frac{C + R + I}{S}$$

Where:

T = trustworthiness
C = credibility
R = reliability
I = intimacy
S = self-orientation

Fig. 8.2. Trust Realms

Component	Realm	Example
Credibility	Words	I can trust what he says about . . .
Reliability	Actions	I can trust her to . . .
Intimacy	Emotions	I feel comfortable discussing this . . .
Self-orientation	Motives	I can trust that he cares about . . .

The answer, of course, is that trust has multiple dimensions. I might trust your expertise, but distrust (profoundly) your motives (i.e., self-orientation). I might trust your brilliance, but dislike your style of dealing with me (your intimacy).

Fig. 8.3. Individual Failings

Poor Marks On:	Get Characterized As:
Credibility	Windbags
Reliability	Irresponsible
Intimacy	Technicians
Self-orientation	Devious

Winning trust requires that you do well on all four dimensions (in the client's eyes), unless you are so *superb* at one or two dimensions that you can overcome some relative weaknesses in the others. Even then, you have to be truly superb, not just good.

One of Rob's children was diagnosed as having a serious medical condition when she was barely three years old. Given the complexity and potential severity of the situation, she was referred to a highly specialized surgeon at Children's Hospital in Boston who was sufficiently famous to have been the subject of a book, written about him and his work, complete with photographs of his hands. From the standpoint of credibility and reliability, few people in the world could match him. But his intimacy skills were not among the highest, to be sure.

This was pointedly obvious when, at the end of six hours of surgery on Rob's daughter, the surgeon emerged from the operating room saying to the anxious parents, "Don't worry. *He's* fine." Rob and his wife, Susan, almost shouted in unison, "She's a she!" He shrugged and casually said, "Oh, yeah, I meant to say 'she.' Anyway, she'll be fine. Complex surgery. Interesting case. We videotaped it." With that, he strolled away, leaving two grateful yet dumbfounded parents in his wake.

Did this surgeon "get away with it?" Yes. Can *you* get by only on technical excellence? Yes, you can, barely, if you're world-famous. The rest of us cannot.

Credibility

It does not diminish the importance of credibility to say that it is the one aspect of trust that is most commonly achieved. Given the focus that most professionals place on their technical expertise, and its relative tangibility, this is the factor most likely to be done well by you (and your competitors).

Credibility isn't just content expertise. It's content expertise plus "presence," which refers to how we look, act, react, and talk about our content. It depends not only on the substantive reality of the advisor's expertise, but also on the *experience* of the person doing the perceiving. As the chapter on relationship building suggested (Chapter 5), we must find ways not only to be credible, but also to give the client the sense that we are credible. We must illustrate, not assert.

Why do doctors hang all those diplomas and certificates on their office walls? The paper on the wall is a shorthand means of communicating both competence and experience, which results in credibility. That impressive, scripted diploma appeals to both our rational and our emotional sides. We see not only certification of certain skills (competence) but also a testimonial from an institution, designed to make us feel good. The net result is aimed at reducing the patient's concerns as they sit half-dressed in a cold examination room.

At the same time, doctors also create credibility in a direct way, either through repeated positive experiences, or from a compelling diagnosis of what is wrong (and what is to be done about it). In either case, we believe the doctor: he or she has the perceived credibility that derives from experience. There are both rational and emotional components at work.

The concept of credibility includes notions of both accuracy and completeness. These parallel the rational and emotional realms. Accuracy, in the client-advisor world, is mostly rational. We check facts, logic, and other people's experiences to assess whether someone is accurate. Completeness, on the other hand, is frequently assessed more emotionally.

When someone is perceived to be accurate, we use the word "believable" to describe them. When we are talking about their completeness, on the other hand, we say they are "honest."

Among the four components of the trust equation, credibility requires a moderate amount of time to establish. For the rational component of credibility (believability) we can examine someone's logic, or check someone's claims against the direct experience of others (i.e., references). This doesn't take long. The emotional side of credibility (honesty) takes longer to evaluate, because it takes longer to assure oneself that all dimensions of an issue are being covered. These relationships are shown in Figure 8-4.

What lessons should an advisor draw from this view of credibility? Primarily that, while most providers sell on the basis of technical competence, most buyers buy on the basis of emotion. Since credibility is the most overtly rational component of the trust equation, it is a natural magnet for professionals seeking to establish trust. However, there is not only a temptation to overemphasize credibility as a component of trust, it is tempting to overemphasize the rational component of credibility itself.

Of course, credibility is important. It is important to get the con-

Fig. 8.4. Comparison of Rational and Emotional Credibility

Realm	Rational	Emotional
Characteristics	Accuracy	Completeness
Response	Believability: not telling lies	Honesty: telling truths, completely
Channel	Testimonial; Direct Experience	Direct Experience

tent right, to convey how smart we are, how well we've thought through the guidance the client is seeking from us. So we tend naturally to spend time on our logic, our facts, and to list our credentials: all direct appeals to rationality.

What we tend *not* to do is to enhance the emotional side of credibility: to convey a sense of honesty, to allay any unconscious suspicions of incompleteness. The best service professionals excel at two things in conveying credibility: anticipating needs, and speaking about needs that are commonly not articulated.

For example, we might ask a client, "Tell me, what was your reaction to your competitor's latest move?" This enhances our credibility by showing that we are knowledgeable or have done our homework. Or, one might use phrases that start with, "You know, I suppose if I were in your position, I might be wondering about X. Is it possible that that is an issue for you?" Again, the delicate "offering" of an insight or piece of content (without assertiveness) allows the client to form a conclusion about our mastery of content and our ability to contribute new perspectives.

Some final tips on enhancing credibility:

1. Figure out how to tell as much truth as possible, except where doing so would injure others.

2. Don't tell lies, or even exaggerate. At all. Ever.

3. Avoid saying things that others might construe as lies. For example, "Yes of course, we'll put our best people on the job." (Really? Who are the worst? Says who? And how come the best don't seem to be very busy?) Or, "We don't write reports that just sit on shelves." (Really? Who are you implying does write such reports? And do you mean you don't give us documentation?)

4. Speak with expression, not monotonically. Use body language, eye contact, and vocal range. Show the client you have energy around the subject at hand.

5. Don't just cite references. Where it is genuinely possible to create mutual benefit, introduce your clients to each other; they will learn from each other, and you will have plenty of reflected credit in which to bask.

6. When you don't know, say so, quickly and directly.

7. Yes it's important to have them know your credentials. It will make them feel better and it will make you feel better. A text bio sent as an advance background sheet is of particular value in new relationships, as well as any article reprints or (flattering) quotes

about you. Just don't get silly by having all those initials and certifications appear after your name on your business card.

8. Relax. You know much more than you think you know. If you don't really belong there, then don't put yourself there in the first place.

9. Make sure you've done absolutely all your homework on the client company, the client marketplace, and the client individual, and that it's absolutely up to the minute. Even if you know them and their business cold, there is likelihood that there will be some news clip about your client that will have been published that very day.

10. There's no reason to show off. They already assume you know what you're talking about (or how to handle a situation). The number of times clients actually want to test your knowledge is actually quite low.

11. Love your topic. It will show.

Reliability

Reliability is about whether clients think you are dependable and can be trusted to behave in consistent ways. Judgments on reliability are strongly affected, if not determined, by the number of times the client has interacted with you. We tend to trust the people we know well, and assign less trustworthiness to those with whom we have not interacted.

If I've dealt with you five or six times in, say, six months, I have a better idea of what to expect from you than if I've known you for a year but have only dealt with you once or twice. Judgments about reliability can be "borrowed" by checking the experiences that other clients have had with the advisor. These are temporary estimates, however, and can be quickly revised by the client's own direct experience.

Reliability is the one component of the trust equation that has an explicit action orientation. It links words and deeds, intention and action. It is this action orientation that distinguishes reliability from credibility.

Reliability in this largely rational sense is the *repeated experience of links between promises and action.* We judge someone's reliability with due dates and quality levels: "on time and on spec." Less formally, we consider the time it takes someone to return a phone call, whether meetings are canceled or kept, and whether to-do lists are completed.

Reliability also has an emotional aspect, which is revealed when things are done in the manner that clients prefer, or to which they are accustomed. We unconsciously form opinions about someone's reliability by the extent to which they seem to anticipate our own habits, expectations, routines, and quirks. These anticipations include whether someone dresses in a manner we consider appropriate, or the phrasing and intonation of someone's speech. Reliability in this emotional sense is *the repeated experience of expectations fulfilled.*

A good advisor will find (or create) a number of opportunities to demonstrate both rational and emotional reliability, by making promises, explicit or implicit, and then delivering on them.

Consider Federal Express, an organization most of us think of as highly reliable. We think of them as reliable partly because their advertising sends us that message, and partly because they deliver on their promise. Yet not all of their reputation for reliability comes from the obvious "technical" aspect of their service offerings.

We experience a sense of reliability from FedEx:

- when we get first-ring responses on their 800 number
- when the voice mail interface is as painless as possible
- when the associate answering the phone is knowledgeable and energetic
- from the consistent look and feel of their packaging
- from the way the zip-strip always tears off the same way
- from the consistent paint job on the trucks
- from the uniforms that distinguish them from other carriers
- from the easy-to-use and accurate "tracking" system
- from the fact that the delivery driver turnover rate is low
- from the driver consistently leaving your package in the same place (the place you want it left)

All these characteristics are consistent and reinforce reliability. In addition, they are tailored to be user-friendly, to fit our own notions of what is familiar. Consistency alone is not enough to create reliability. It must also be consistency in terms of the client's preferences, not just the provider's.

How does reliability play out in professional services? Advisors who rate the highest on reliability will not just deliver their work on time and on spec. Nor will they simply be consistent, even at a level of excellence.

They will also be expert at a variety of small touches that are aimed at client-based familiarity. Sending meeting material in advance is one example; staying current on client events and names is another. Reliability on the emotional level has a great deal to do with the client's preferences, and not just with consistency from the service provider's perspective.

Strategies for reliability include setting up a series of deadlines or opportunities to deliver discrete work product components within a short and usually agreed-upon period of time. The biggest leverage for reliability enhancement probably lies in the emotional realm. The more a provider can do to understand and relate to the usually unconscious norms of the client, the more the client will feel at ease and experience a sense of reliability.

Some final thoughts on reliability:

1. Make specific commitments to your client around small things: getting that article by tomorrow, placing the call, writing the draft by Monday, looking up a reference. And then deliver on them, quietly, and on time.

2. Send meeting materials in advance so that the client has the option of reviewing them in advance, saving meeting time for substantive discussions.

3. Make sure meetings have clear goals, not just agendas, and ensure the goals are met.

4. Use the client's "fit and feel" around terminology, style, formats, hours.

5. Review agendas with your client, before meetings, before phone calls, before discussions. Clients should know that they can expect you to always solicit their views on how time will be spent.

6. Reconfirm scheduled events before they happen. Announce changes to scheduled or committed dates *as soon as* they change.

Intimacy

The most effective, as well as the most common, sources of differentiation in trustworthiness come from intimacy and self-orientation. Both of these are relatively scarce, compared to credibility and reliability. People trust those with whom they are willing to talk about difficult agendas (intimacy), and those who demonstrate that they care (low self-orientation).

The most common failure in building trust is the lack of intimacy. Some professionals consider it a positive virtue to maintain an emotional distance from their clients. They work hard at being "aloof." We believe that they do so not only at their own risk but also their clients'.

Business can be intensely personal. There are obvious human emotions around such charged issues as promotion, compensation, hiring and firing, reorganization, and other forms of decision making. The same emotional environment surrounds the "macro" business environment: mergers and acquisitions, lawsuits, changing pension plans, selling off businesses, and closing down plants are all areas that go well beyond logic. Hundreds, if not thousands, of lives are affected by these activities. It should be no surprise, then, that intimacy is needed to make a connection to the interior, emotional state of the client.

We don't mean that private lives necessarily get shared via intimacy. We do mean that things personal, related to the issues at hand, get shared. It is possible to have an intimate relationship with a client, in the sense that we mean it here, and not have anything to do with their life outside work. Intimacy is about "emotional closeness" concerning the issues at hand, so it is obviously the most overtly emotional of the four trust equation components. It is driven by emotional honesty, a willingness to expand the bounds of acceptable topics, while maintaining mutual respect and by respecting boundaries. Greater intimacy means that fewer subjects are barred from discussion.

Establishing intimacy is playing a "game" of mutually increasing risk. One party offers a piece of himself or herself and the other party either responds (thereby deepening intimacy), or chooses not to respond (thereby drawing an intimacy line). Behaving appropriately requires knowing when to take a risk, and knowing when a risk has been declined and how to behave in the face of the declination.

We should recognize that clumsy attempts to establish intimacy too soon could backfire. Perhaps it comes from a vendor who assumes we share his passion for golf; or a dinner invitation we put off with "Yes, let's do that, sometime," or a sharing of personal experiences that is more information than we want to know.

The fear of committing this kind of gaffe (assuming more intimacy than is desired) is a very great fear for a very great number of service professionals. Intimacy is scary stuff. Of all the components of trust, it's the one that seems so easy to get so wrong. We like to believe we can control or influence credibility. We know our content, or at least we know what we don't know. We can demonstrate reliability. We can even get comfortable with keeping self-orientation low if we focus on the other person instead of ourselves.

But intimacy? Now that's another matter. It's the one element that seems to have such high consequences if we get it wrong, because we run the risk of being publicly exposed and personally vulnerable. Intimacy is more about who *we are* than any other aspect of trust.

Creating intimacy is a dance, requiring some cautious stepping and some leaps of faith that bad things won't happen as one makes new, carefully selected moves. Here are a few suggestions:

1. *Be not afraid!* Creating intimacy requires courage, not just for you, but for everyone. Chances are, you've had at least some degree of success in forming intimate relationships at some time in your life. It's the same thing here.

2. *People in senior positions appreciate candor, but candor isn't necessarily intimacy, and they value that even more.* Senior people get coddled a lot. Messages to them are often polished to the point of unrecognizability prior to their delivery.

   We know a CEO who is liberated by the fact that his senior people all tell him the truth. But that's not all. There is also intimacy between them. They know each other well enough to be able to get angry with each other, to call each other's bluff, to challenge each other's thinking on a regular basis. The CEO looks for that same trait in his outside advisors, and if it is lacking, he is not averse to switching advisors. Of course, one must learn to disagree without being disagreeable!

3. *Find the fun and fascination.* By getting closer to the emotional components of the client's decision making, we can ask people questions they haven't previously heard from advisors. It shows we have a different angle, a different point of view, and a broader perspective. It's fun for them and it's fun for us. It builds rapport and repartee. And you learn a lot.

4. *Test whether you're coming too close to the line, or pushing too far, too fast.* Ask yourself if you were in your client's position, would this topic be something you'd want to talk about with someone you trusted? If the answer is yes, you're most of the way there. But not completely. You also want to make sure that it's the right topic, right time, and right phrasing of the question.

   Think of how you're posing it, or planning to pose it. Have you given your client a reasonable way *not* to answer the question? People need a readily accessible, face-saving "out" if they don't want to (or are not ready to) answer. If you can't say yes to both parts of this, you're too close to the line.

5. *Practice a little.* No, you can't practice spontaneity, but you can practice phrasing. Rob often writes down two or three ways of asking difficult questions or delivering difficult messages, testing and trying them out before actually using them.

6. *Don't Overrate the Downside Risk.* What exactly are you afraid of? Sometimes we're afraid of saying something because we think it will put the business at risk. But if we're honest, we often find what is at risk isn't the business itself, it is our own personal comfort with expanding the bounds of intimacy. The business risk is often overstated. And paradoxically, the way to manage the business risk is often to take what feels like the personal risk.

7. *One of You Has to Make the First Move. And It's You!* Increased intimacy starts with one person or another taking what feels like a personal risk, to share something of what they see, feel or think about something. If that risk is met in kind, intimacy is increased, and thus trust is increased. It is an endless and useless internal debate to believe that the client should make the first move in this dance. You as the professional have no control over that other person. The only actions you can influence are your own. Accept responsibility for being the first risk-taker.

Will all of this, put together, give you immediate powers of intimacy building? No, but we hope it will get you started. Many professionals assume that intimacy always takes the longest time to develop among the trust factors. This is not so. In fact, done well, it is potentially the least time-dependent component.

Rob was working with a company that had just reorganized. One of the executives, historically considered a high flyer, felt there was no longer a place for him in the organization. No one had come and spoken personally to him about it. The honest truth was that the person was still held in high regard, but no one had told him that. Tears flowed during Rob's conversation with this man.

Of course, Rob felt uncomfortable, but that's not the point. What was required was only to give this man a chance to vent, and to acknowledge that the situation was uncomfortable. In so doing, Rob gave him a chance to keep talking, and to navigate his way through the period of uncertainty.

We are not required to solve the client's emotional state, but it is a major step forward in a trust relationship when a client can feel comfortable enough to express strong emotion. Imagine how much weaker the substantive business relationship would have been if this client had never revealed his inner state to Rob.

Self-Orientation

There is no greater source of distrust than advisors who appear to be more interested in themselves than in trying to be of service to the client. We must work hard to show that our self-orientation is under control.

The most egregious form of self-orientation is, of course, simple selfishness, being "in it for the money." However, self-orientation is about much more than greed. It covers anything that keeps us focused on ourselves rather than on our client. The following list reveals how many "threats" there are to client focus (and temptations for self-orientation):

1. Selfishness
2. Self-consciousness
3. A need to appear on top of things
4. A desire to look intelligent
5. A to-do list on our mind that is a mile long
6. A desire to jump to the solution
7. A desire to win that exceeds the desire to help the client
8. A desire to be right
9. A desire to be seen to be right
10. A desire to be seen as adding value

11. Fears of various kinds: of not knowing, of not having the right answer, of not appearing intelligent, of being rejected

In short, any form of preoccupation with our own agenda is focusing on something other than the client, and it will reduce trust directly.

Clients recognize excessive self-orientation through such things as:

1. A tendency to relate their stories to ourselves
2. A need to too quickly finish their sentences for them
3. A need to fill empty spaces in conversations
4. A need to appear clever, bright, witty, etc.
5. An inability to provide a direct answer to a direct question
6. An unwillingness to say we don't know
7. Name-dropping of other clients
8. A recitation of qualifications
9. A tendency to give answers too quickly
10. A tendency to want to have the last word
11. Closed-ended questions early on
12. Putting forth hypotheses or problem statements before fully hearing the client's hypotheses or problem statements
13. Passive listening; a lack of visual and verbal cues that indicate the client is being heard
14. Watching the client as if he/she were a television set (merely a source of data)

How do we, as would-be trusted advisors, demonstrate a lack of self-orientation? Through the following kinds of behaviors (which both represent and help create an inner state of client focus):

1. Letting the client fill in the empty spaces
2. Asking the client to talk about what's behind an issue
3. Using open-ended questions
4. Not giving answers until the right is earned to do so (and the client will let you know when you have earned it)
5. Focusing on defining the problem, not guessing the solution

6. Reflective listening, summarizing what we've heard to make sure we heard correctly what was said and what was intended

7. Saying you don't know when you don't know

8. Acknowledging the feelings of the client (with respect)

9. Learning to tell the client's story before we write our own

10. Listening to clients without distractions: door closed, phone off, email not in line of sight, frequent eye contact

11. Resisting with confidence a client's invitation to provide a solution too early on—to stay in the listening and joint problem definition phases of discussion

12. Trusting in our ability to add value *after* listening, rather than trying to do so *during* listening

13. Taking most of the responsibility for failed communications

Here are some additional ways of making sure self-orientation stays low:

Talk to your client as if he or she is a friend. Even if clients are *not* actually our friends, we can be friendly with them. Our conversational tone and tenor can be (we would argue, *has* to be) one of friendship. We're concerned about our friends and their well-being, and it shows in our conversational style. We should use the same style with clients.

Think about how you would help your client if you were responsible for this person's future success. Even if you are a specialist called in only on specific occasions, think about their success. Try to make their concerns *your* concerns.

Pay attention. Having low self-orientation requires intensely personal attention. This doesn't mean focusing endless hours on each client or potential client. But it does mean starting each interaction, each analysis, each project in an intensely one-to-one manner.

Be honest with yourself about your level of interest. If, over time, you feel little interest in the work, it will be hard to keep your self-orientation low. If you're not interested or inspired by the work or the client, it's almost inevitable that you will focus more on yourself. But if that's happening too often, it's time to make a change to work that interests you more, either new clients or new matters. If you have any choice, you know that life is too short to work on the uninspiring.

Being on the receiving end of dealing with someone with low self-orientation can be an amazing experience. More than twenty years ago, Mary Doyle, most recently Counsel to the Secretary of the Interior, was one of Rob's law professors. Rob still remembers a Saturday lunch with her and the time she spent with him a few weeks before his first set of law school finals.

He remembers the intense focus she had on the conversation and the topics at hand. It was as if nothing else mattered in the world. She made it clear that the conversation would go *where* he wanted it to go, and for *as long as* he wanted it to go.

Although she might not have realized it at the time, it was one of the most profoundly helpful conversations he ever had. Part of it was indeed the sound advice being offered, but an equally significant part was the intensity of her commitment to help him resolve what needed to be resolved.

Trust and Relationship Economics

Is this trust stuff just so much softness? Absolutely not! It's profitable. The trust equation is useful in clarifying the economics of client relationships. By assigning values to the four factors, the equation can be used to assess the trust level of a relationship, which might be particularly useful to you in comparing different relationships.

We will contrast the relationship of a professional with a new client and with a client of long standing.

In the new client case, we might rate the client's initial perception of the professional's credibility as 5 on a scale of 1 to 10, perhaps based on reputation and very early perceptions. Reliability, which typically takes longer to establish, might be rated as a 3, and intimacy, which certainly takes more time to establish, might be given a 2.

The client's perception of the professional's degree of self-orientation in a new client setting might be an 8. This reflects the fact that a common starting assumption by a client, based on past experience, is that the professional is primarily interested in looking after his or her own interests. That view might change once the client gets to know the professional, but a low self-orientation is rarely the starting assumption.

We therefore get:

New Client

$$(C+R+I)/S = (5+3+2)/8 = 10/8 = 1.25$$

Now let's look at a reasonably successful existing client relationship, where the numerator's values will be higher, and the denominator lower.

Existing Client

$$(C+R+I)/S = (7+8+5)/4 = 20/4 = 5$$

(If you think our guesses or estimates are off, substitute your own. It's a simple calculation.) Our calculations are summarized in Figure 8-5.

The ratio of our two scenarios (in this case the ratio between 5 and 1.25, or 4) is of economic interest. Like many other researchers, we have found in our work with professional service firms that the cost of developing new-client business is 4 to 7 times higher than the cost of developing the same amount of business from an existing client. The trust equation gives us a major insight into why this is so, and what might be done about it.

This ratio between "undeveloped" and "developed" trust closely parallels that between highly profitable and highly unprofitable businesses. High-retention relationships are high-trust relationships. A trust-based strategy is a profitable strategy.

Fig. 8.5. Our Calculations

Component	Credibility	Reliability	Intimacy	Self-Orientation	Calculation	Trust Factor
New Client	5	3	2	8	$\frac{10}{8}$	1.25
Existing Client	7	8	5	4	$\frac{20}{4}$	5
Ratio						4:0

9

The Development of Trust

IN THIS CHAPTER, we introduce a new set of concepts that build on (but are different from) those we have discussed thus far. Starting here, we begin an in-depth, multichapter investigation of the stages of building trust, in an attempt to provide a structure for understanding trust development.

We suggest that there are five distinct steps in the development of a trusted relationship. In this chapter we will define each of these stages. In the succeeding chapters, we will explore each stage in detail.

Expressed in their simplest form, the five stages are:

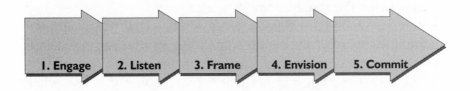

Figure 9-1 on page 86 summarizes, at each stage in the trust process, what the client is primarily feeling, and what the advisor gains at the successful completion of each step.

Engage

Engagement, the first stage of building trust, is the point in the process where the client begins to feel two things: (1) There is an

Fig. 9.1 Summary of the Trust Process

Trust Process Step	Action Taken	What the Client Feels	What the Advisor Gains
1. Engage	Attention becomes focused	"It may be worth talking to this person about . . ."	Earns the right to tell and hear truths
2. Listen	Ears bigger than mouth; acknowledge and affirm	"I am being both heard and understood . . ."	Earns the right to suggest a problem statement or definition
3. Frame	The root issue is stated clearly and openly	"Yes, that is exactly the problem here . . ."	Coalesces issues to move forward
4. Envision	A vision of an alternate reality is sketched out	"Could we really accomplish that? That could be a really interesting outcome."	Concretizes vision; generates clarity of objectives.
5. Commit	Steps are agreed upon; sense of commitment is renewed	"I agree, I understand what needs to be done. I'm with you, let's do it."	Allows problem-resolution to begin.

issue worth talking about; and (2) This person is worth talking to on that issue.

There must be both elements to create engagement. We have all had experiences where clients are willing to talk to us but will not acknowledge the issue as important to them. We have also had clients, even long-term clients, who acknowledged new issues but thought we were not the people to speak to about them. Obviously, neither situation represented successful "engagement."

Note that engaging is not just a process that you use when meeting new client prospects for the first time. It is just as important, if not even more so, to reengage in relationships that grow to cover new client needs. In both cases, new and existing, we as advisors must demonstrate to the client that we are worthy of being spoken to in an open, truthful manner about the issue at hand.

Listen

Listening, when successful, is the stage in the process where the client comes to believe that the advisor understands him or her. The purpose of listening in building trust is to *earn the right* to engage in a mutual exploration of ideas.

Good listening must be active, incisive, conscious, involved, and interactive. But good listening only begins with these things.

The successful professional will listen for what is said *and* what is unspoken. In addition, it is necessary to confirm and validate what we have heard. We must not only listen; we must do something to give the client the *experience* of having been listened to. This is vital to earning the right to move forward.

Frame

Successful framing, which is simultaneously a means of building trust and an essential part of giving advice, is the process by which the advisor helps the client crystallize and clarify the many issues involved in the client's problem. Framing consists of formulating problem statements, hypotheses, and points of view, built around what is important to the client. Framing is usually the point in the process where the client becomes consciously aware of value being added by the advisor, and hence where significant levels of trust can be built.

As we shall see in Chapter 12, the advisor's clarification of the issues may be rational or may involve redefining the client's issues in a political or emotional framework. Framing is rarely an *exclusively* logical or rational process. The purpose of framing is to reveal and organize the client's issues and to help the understanding of the problem (by all parties involved) coalesce into a common view, so that the process can move forward with greater clarity and solidarity.

Envision

Having defined the problem, some might think that the next logical step is to solve it. We don't think so. Any problem can have many solutions, depending upon what the client wants to achieve, or for which future state he or she wants to aim. The role of joint envisioning in the trust development process is to concretize a specific vision (and choice) among possible future states.

By jointly envisioning, the advisor and the client imagine (in rich detail) how the end result might look, without prematurely giving in to the temptation to solve the problem.

Envisioning entails addressing (at least) the following questions?

1. What are we *really* aiming for here?
2. What will it look like when we get there?
3. How will we know we are there?

In the envisioning process, the advisor might say:

"I know you want to live a healthier life, and we can certainly help, but how much exercise do you envision doing? Do you want to lose ten pounds or thirty pounds? What's the expectation here? We can't help you until we have explored all the implications of your choice, and understand which vision you want to pursue. Do you really want to aim to both lose thirty pounds and give up smoking? Are you certain that's what your goal is? Are you *ready* to achieve it? Do you wish to lower the bar before making a commitment? Make sure you are not setting yourself up to fail."

Notice that sometimes the advisor may add value by getting the client to expand his or her dreams (aim high), but sometimes envisioning requires the advisor to manage down the client's expectations, based on the knowledge of the advisor about what is and is not achievable.

When done successfully, envisioning is usually the point in the process where the client begins to understand his or her own true goals and defines them so that he or she can realistically be committed to achieving them. It should be recognized that sometimes, even acknowledged problems remain unresolved, as a matter of the client's choice. The client may determine that the benefits of the future state are not worth the effort, and that she or he can live with the problem. (We're not all fit and slim!)

Commit

Just as in losing weight, a client may understand the problem, urgently desire the end state, but be unsure not only about what it takes to get there, but whether or not he or she has the will to do what it takes to achieve the vision.

The purpose of the commitment stage of trust building (and advice giving) is to ensure that the client understands (in all of its rational, emotional, and political complexity) what it will take to achieve the vision, and to help the client find the determination to do what is necessary.

What follows from commitment is action (by the client or the advisor). The advisor must make sure that expectations have been managed thoroughly. Only through a detailed commitment process can the advisor know what to do. Only when there is commitment will the client have the trust and confidence that the advisor is doing what the client wants.

The added value of this stage is to help the client understand what it will take to solve the problem, and the trust building comes from the candor with which the advisor lays out the challenges and risks involved. ("These people are being straight with me, unlike those other people who promise the moon and pretend they can solve everything.")

Another Look

Here's another way of looking at the five stages:

1. Engage: Uses language of interest and concern

    "I've been thinking about your competitors, and . . ."

    "Your people have been telling me about . . ."

2. Listen: Uses language of understanding and empathy

    "Tell me more about . . ."

    "What's behind that?"

    "Gosh, that must feel . . ."

3. Frame: Uses language of perspective and candor

    "I see three key themes emerging here . . ."

    "You know, what's tough to do here is . . ."

4. Envision: Uses language of possibility

    "Wouldn't it be great if . . ."

5. Commit: Uses language of joint exploration

    "What would it take, for each of us, to . . ."

Skills Required

The five stages of trust building have very different emotional overtones, and they require different skills on the part of the trustee to accomplish.

1. Engaging requires the skill of being (credibly) noticed.
2. Listening requires an ability to *understand* another human being.
3. Framing requires creative insight and emotional courage.
4. Envisioning requires a spirit of collaboration and creativity.
5. Commitment requires the ability to generate enthusiasm, and sometimes the ability to manage down overenthusiasm.

It is natural for all of us to have a tendency to lead with our particular strengths. This tendency also holds true of people's view of the trust development process. One of our clients (a strategy consulting firm) when presented with the five-step, trust-building model, said, "You know, the highest-payoff, highest-probability step in that process (the one that results in increasing trust more than all the other steps) is the framing step."

A different firm (for example, one in the change management business) might point to listening and envisioning as being the key steps. Still another firm might point to engagement, getting the client's focused attention around an issue, as the magic button.

However, no one step is "key." All are essential to the trust-development process. The point in the process at which a client might articulate a "key moment" depends very much on the issue being discussed, and especially on the approach of the advisor.

In the following chapters, we shall examine each of the five steps in more detail, and offer suggestions on how to execute each of them.

10

Engagement

ENGAGEMENT, THE FIRST STEP in trust building, is the stage where it first occurs to the client that maybe, perhaps, somehow, the person standing here in front of him or her might be able to help in finding a solution to a (specific) problem. This can happen in either a new or existing client situation.

Many advisors believe that the trust-building process begins with listening. But something else must come first, before a (new or existing) client will actually start to talk about a need. That something involves an initial connection between the advisor and the client. We call it engaging.

For a client, engagement is a nontrivial decision. Whatever issue the client faces, it will require some emotional energy, and personal risk, just to put it forth. This is not done unless a decision is made to invest time and energy, and to take a risk, which isn't taken unless the potential client sees some likelihood of good results.

Clients have lots of people who want their time. We recently heard a prominent chief financial officer talk to a group of accounting partners about what he seeks in an advisor. He started off by saying that people from accounting and consulting firms were constantly trying to get on his calendar, and that they had better have something valuable to offer. Unfortunately, too many come in "just asking me what my problems are and wanting to listen. They bring nothing of value to the meeting."

Clients don't open up just because we listen, not even existing clients. They have to think we're worth talking to *on this issue.* Some trigger has to be pulled in the mind of the client so that he or she will open up to *us,* in particular. Think about your own experiences. To whom do you open up? Who opens up to you?

How can we get a client to engage? Shock or surprise can be used to alter the ongoing perceptions and expectations that have become habitual in the relationship. Service firms in recent years have become slightly more daring in their willingness to use surprises, or to alter expectations, albeit quite within socially acceptable bounds.

Engaging with New Clients

We referred in Chapter 3 to the use of saddlebags and pizza boxes as a way of getting the client's attention and demonstrating initiative and creativity. Without wishing to overstress these examples, they illustrate the principle that being seen as *visibly trying to customize* our activities to this specific client, doing something a little different to communicate a message and gain attention, is potentially very powerful.

We don't just mean powerful in a self-oriented sales sense, but in the sense of building the beginnings of trust. By showing we are willing to enter the client's world, however symbolically, we create a feeling in the client of:

> "Maybe these people aren't like all the others. These people are really trying to earn and deserve my attention. They've earned the right, at least, for me to proceed to the next step of speaking with them."

That's (the beginnings of) trust building.

Other methods of visibly customizing include presenting your messages in the format used on the client's Internet or Web site. Perhaps you could incorporate clients' products in interesting ways into your communications. We have heard of the successful use of videos, audios, and even live acting performances by professionals, all techniques to shake up the existing patterns of perception, ways to get the client to engage anew.

If you have the time, or a research department to back you up, you can learn a great deal about prospective clients and their issues from trade magazines, trade associations, and, of course, the Internet. This approach works wonderfully with new clients. One major consulting firm built its success on a strategy of carefully selecting the target new clients it pursued, and before making even the first contact with the target client, it did a thorough analysis of the industry. It did not just collect the facts, but truly did an analysis and developed insights and a point of view. They would then approach their target and say:

> "We have some unique insights into your industry and we'd like to come and share them with you, for free. We don't pretend to know your business as well as you do, but we think we've got some information and views that are a little different. May we come and discuss them with you?"

This is another example of earning sales by earning trust, and earning trust by the principles set forth in Chapter 5 on relationship building: Go first, illustrate, and don't assert.

In the book *You're Working Too Hard to Make the Sale,* Bill Brooks and Tom Travesano suggest that advisors need to indicate quickly that they understand the buyer's wants. Not needs. Wants. And not even deliver, just understand. In other words, we must engage quickly around something that is really meaningful to the client.

Why does this work as an attention getter? Because it is so rare that an advisor truly succeeds in getting out of his or her own internally based worldview to put forth a client-focused view of the world.

We are too often worried about ourselves, and it shows. We worry about our lines, we rehearse our presentation, we check our appearance, and we fine-tune our proposal's text. All are activities that are self-oriented, not focused on the other person. When an advisor succeeds in breaking through the clutter and clearly articulating something that is genuinely and accurately aimed at the client's wants, it is striking. Striking enough to create engagement.

(Re-)Engaging with Existing Clients

In an interesting parallel to our earlier discussion on romance and relationship building, questions arise as to the engagement process with clients of long standing. How does one reengage with an existing client? How can we be fresh and captivating over longer periods of time, or after multiple assignments? How do we do this and not be perceived as being too predictable (and our motives being distrusted)?

In the early stages of relationship building (in business or personal life), it is partially the new, the intriguing, and the exciting things that got the relationship started. In an ongoing relationship, being able to get clients to open up means doing or saying things that are still sufficiently new, intriguing, and exciting.

Existing clients generally give us the opportunity for an audience. They'll give us a chance, they'll hear us out, they'll nod appropriately. The deeper question, however, is whether they'll engage and open. They don't always do so. We've all had the slightly unnerving experience of having gone to a client to talk about what we believe could be a hot issue or of great interest to them only to be met by blank stares.

With an existing client, you might say:

> "Susan, I've been looking at your Web site and those of your competitors, and I notice that many of your competitors are making some very significant moves. I certainly don't have the answers, but I do have some thoughts about how you might respond. Would you, or your team, like to get together to bat around some ideas? No charge, of course. I don't want to stick my nose in where it's not wanted, but if you'd like my thoughts I'd be happy to share them."

Successful approaches often (but not always) derive from the prior knowledge you have gained on preceding client work or in earlier client conversations. Here are some examples, and some specific phrasings that accompany them. Note the emphases, and what they connote:

1. Approaches that demonstrate concern about competitive developments

   "I'm a little *worried* about how your competitor is raising its profile in the marketplace, and wanted to talk to you about it."

2. Approaches that signal an understanding of career challenges facing a particular individual

   "I've been watching what's been going on here with [for example] succession and succession planning, and how that might *affect your decision-making.*"

3. Approaches that might offer a solution to a specific managerial issue

"A while ago, you mentioned *you were concerned* about how [for example] the two groups would integrate, and I wanted to share some observations."

4. Approaches that demonstrate continuity and development

"I've thought a lot about *something you said* four weeks ago."

These are competitive, career, or personal issues. They contrast with more content- or expertise-driven approaches, most of which prevail in the earlier stages of client relationships. In those earlier stages, advisors have not yet earned the right (nor might they have the knowledge) to go in and start discussing the career challenges of a particular client. Later on, however, it is a more appropriate topic for conversation.

Engaging with existing clients is not just about topic. It's also about timing. After we have gathered information that may be valuable in helping craft a new client discussion, it's essential to further evaluate the attempt to engage on the bases of urgency and importance.

Steven Covey has long made use of the critical differences between urgency and importance in much of his work on personal effectiveness. It also has great relevance here. We all know how annoying it is to be asked to address topics of great importance when we don't have the time to consider them.

Engaging with existing clients is about picking the right topic at the right time. We have limited opportunities for time with them, and if we choose poorly, our opportunities get even fewer. Here are two quick rules of thumb that we have found useful:

First, introduce the topics in an order that relates to the amount of time available with the client. (Its always amazing that some people don't even check to see how much time the client has available.) If you have only a limited amount of time (a pass-in-the-hall, or five minutes), lay out the agenda, start with the urgent, and end with the important (even if it's just a phrase or thought to come back to at some later point). If you have somewhat more time, start with the important, and save five minutes at the end of the conversation for the urgent. Either way, it will buy you more client time.

Second, don't hold back in raising a topic. Even if you can't cover it all or show how brilliant you are, it's still worthwhile to raise it. We never have enough time to show how much we know or how much we care, but offering even an indication of our caring for a client can put us in very good stead, even years later.

Engaging New Clients

Engaging a new client isn't just luck. You can improve your luck considerably by doing the following:

Find out absolutely everything you can about your new potential client. Anybody who doesn't do a fairly extensive Internet and literature search (not a snoop, mind you, but a search) on both the entity and the individual is missing an easy bet. Follow that up with second-stage research, or the "six degrees of separation" approach: Do you know somebody who knows somebody who might know somebody who used to work with this person?

Make sure that you have at least two or three things that you'd like to talk about with them. Not questions, but topics. The danger here is making sure you haven't picked an overused or stale topic. Some information or a point of view (especially an unpublished one) on competitors or adversaries is almost always of interest.

Figure out whether you might have (or be) something of interest to them, something that they might want to discuss.

You can drop facts or hints about where you've been, or what you've worked on that might be of interest to them, as long as you don't come across as a name-dropper. Just because your brother-in-law's cousin painted Michael Jordan's portrait doesn't qualify, unless you're talking to a sports artist. Make sure it's of interest to them.

Don't make early interactions purely transactional. If you focus strictly on the content, you'll be pegged more as a technician than as an advisor. Talk to them as if they are a *new* friend, not an old friend. There's a difference. There's nothing worse than someone pretending to be overly familiar. Make it conversational enough so they'd want to spend more time together, not less.

Just having a meeting isn't enough. If you can't add value, postpone the meeting. Wait until you *can* add value. It will be worth the wait.

11

The Art of Listening

JACK WELCH, CEO of General Electric, has high praise for Steven Volk, a corporate lawyer to whom Welch turned when GE's subsidiary NBC acquired Financial News Network in 1991. "He is really a great advisor," says Welch. "He listens better than anybody else."

Effective trusted advisors are (without a single exception, in our experience) very good listeners. Listening is not a sufficient condition by itself, but it is a necessary one, the second step in our five-stage process.

Listening is essential to "earn the right" to comment on and be involved with the client's issues. We must listen effectively, and be *perceived* to be listening effectively, *before* we can proceed with any advisory process. Cutting to the chase without having earned the right to do so will usually be interpreted as arrogance.

Listening: Earning the Right

Jim Copeland is the CEO of Deloitte & Touche, and someone who very effectively builds lasting, deep relationships. In 1989, Deloitte, Haskins & Sells merged with Touche, Ross & Co. Copeland had been with Deloitte. He describes the first five minutes of a nine-hour meeting with the CEO of a key Touche, Ross client, a fiery character, who was not at all pleased at having to "train" a whole new accounting firm.

> "He leads with power, energy, wants to overwhelm you, to let you know who's in charge. And I didn't fight that, I just kept saying

'tell me more about that problem, how did it happen, how did it come about, what's going on?' I wanted to know why he was upset, and what it would take to fix things. Basically I was there for him, and let him know that. You just start with an attitude that, by gosh, you are going to set things right, and to do that you have to totally focus on the client and the client's problems."

There are many aspects of Copeland's demeanor in this meeting that explain why it was the genesis of a very long and successful relationship. But in that first meeting, none mattered more than his ability to listen. Listening earned him the right to deliver on quality content, to cross-sell, to demonstrate problem-solving capabilities, and to speak about his people. None of that would have happened had he not earned the right through listening (thereby finding out what was going on.)

Why is "being listened to" so important? The answer is not only about the need for a rational understanding of the issues. Our desire to be heard also flows from our need for respect, empathy, and involvement. The trusted advisor recognizes this, and always ensures that the self-esteem of the client is protected.

A trusted advisor might say, "What I like about your idea is X; now help me understand how we can use it to accomplish Y." Through such language, the advisor constantly lets the client know that the client is respected and that the two of them are free to discuss with great candor the specific merits of the idea at hand.

In listening to earn the right, we have found advisors make two common mistakes. One is to listen only for the rational; the other is to listen too passively.

Overly Rational Listening

The concept of "earning the right" may sound like a rational approach. After all, we send résumés in order to "earn the right" to interview. We send our firm's qualifications to "earn the right" to bid on a piece of work. The truth is, these rational processes only mimic the real action.

Listening to earn the right is very much an emotional as well as a rational process. Here's the rest of Copeland's story.

"So he got the message that I cared about him, and wouldn't let things go by that weren't right for him. Years later, we had a chance to pitch a project to him, $5M, a pretty big project in those days, and at the end of the pitch, he just looked at me and said 'Do *you* think I should do this?'

"Meaning that if I could look him in the eye and say 'you bet' then he had me on the line to do the right thing for him. And he knew that if I didn't believe that, I wouldn't look him in the eye and say so, because he knew he could trust me. And I was able to say, in this case, 'absolutely you should do it; you need this, and we'll do great work for you.'"

We have had clients (and you probably have, too) who insist that this listening stuff is all so much soft talk. "I want results, hard stuff, answers," they insist to us, "don't give me the passive, listening stuff."

Yet at the end of the day, that client (and nearly all clients) wants to be able to look someone in the eye and know that that someone cares for him and won't "let things go by that [aren't] right for him." Is that "soft?" We don't think so.

Overly Passive Listening

The other (related) common mistake in listening to earn the right is to listen too passively. Tony Alessandra, in his audiotape *The Dynamics of Effective Listening,* has a section titled "Giving the Gift of Acknowledgment." We would add, not only is it a gift, it is also a requirement. Good listening is active, not passive.

A key part of communication is the continual back and forth of acknowledging that each is being heard and understood. We all know the blank "uh-huh" and glazed-over look that comes from someone who we just *know* is not really listening to us.

We need, in a normal conversation, some kind of acknowledgment from the other party on a regular basis. Without that, we are forced to stop and either demand it, or stop our communicating.

But what is considered acknowledgment? Is it body language? Words? The answer is that it depends on the content of the message.

If the message is purely rational (for example, a senior lawyer imparting the fine points of an analysis to an associate), then the appropriate acknowledgment may be almost entirely verbal. An occasional "mm-hmm," with a slight nod of the head, is enough to let a teacher know he or she is being heard and understood, and should continue.

But if the message carries any emotional flavor at all (and most do), then *not* to use emotive colorings or tones in our acknowledgments sends the message that we are not listening.

A client who says "We do 300,000 transactions a day here" has a feeling about that number. It is not enough to know whether 300,000 is above or below the competition, or higher or lower than last month. The client may be proud of that number, or proud simply of knowing it. Or he may be bored by the number, or embarrassed by it, or any number of things.

The advisor who listens passively (using only "mm-hmm") is sending a message that only the rational content matters, that the feelings of the one conveying the information are irrelevant. The effective advisor knows that the emotional data is every bit as valid and important as the rational data. Each plays its role in successfully adding value and changing a client organization.

There are even circumstances when a reaction from the advisor is not just good to have, but essential. For example, a CEO who complains that a former key employee is selling trade secrets to the enemy deserves more than mere "mm-hmm." The advisor might appropriately respond as follows:

> "You must be outraged. I wish I had a button to push to resolve this for you instantly, but I don't. I don't think anyone does."

Listening to the Sequence

We have often conducted a real-time quiz to assess the frequency with which people's minds wander from the subject at hand. Our nonscientific study suggests that, on average, business people can pay attention for no more than thirty to sixty seconds without being distracted by an unrelated thought. Listening is a process that requires skill and discipline.

Much of communication follows the model of a story. There is a beginning, a middle, and an end. There is setup, tension, and resolution. There is background, setup, and punch line. When we talk to someone (about almost anything), we choose our words to create some version of a story.

But if the listener breaks up our sense of story (insists on interrupting, or rearranging, or imposing his or her own sense of story line), the meaning we intend is disrupted. It feels inappropriate when someone jumps to a conclusion, or misses a connection, or gets things out of sequence. All these are forms of not "getting it." Good listening respects the speaker by respecting the sequence of the story he or she chooses to tell us.

Our good friends at the Ariel Group, a theater-based communications-training firm in Cambridge, Massachusetts, teach the idea of "reflective listening," followed by "supportive listening," and finally "listening for possibility."

1. Reflective listening demonstrates clarity and communicates back to the speaker that his or her message has been heard and that the impact, implications, and emotions that are connected with the issue are also well understood. ("What I hear you saying is . . .")

2. Supportive listening demonstrates empathy and shows that the listener not only understands why the client feels a particular way about an issue or problem but also that he or she will help the client feel comfortable with that point of view. ("Gee, that must be tough!")

3. Listening for possibility demonstrates insight and suggests to the client that a particular path or solution may help resolve the dilemma. ("So what have you thought about doing to deal with that?")

If we listen sequentially, we will hear the meaning the speaker intends. If we impose our own structure on what is being said, we will not hear the meaning that is being presented. We will hear some version of our own meaning, superimposed on the speaker.

Avoid asking questions such as, "What are the top three issues facing XYZ?" If you ask that question, you'll generally get your list of three. You may, however, miss the fact that one of those issues is far less significant than the other two, and that any unprompted question would have elicited only the two important issues.

Consider the situation of interviewing people you are thinking of hiring for your firm. When you interview candidates by asking them about their capabilities, you deprive them of the chance to tell you their very personal story. If you listen for their story, you will hear the meaning that *they* see in their lives and careers, not one that you may have assigned. You still have the right, of course, to hire or not to hire, but it makes sense to hear someone's idea about what makes them tick before forming your own opinions.

This is as true with clients as it is with interview candidates. If we conduct fact-finding sessions based on rigidly preconceived notions of the issues, we will miss the stories, the meaning, that our clients want to tell us. And thus we miss truth.

Finally, the need to listen to the sequence, and to avoid prematurely imposing our own structure, is even more important in selling than in delivery. If we set an agenda in advance and never move off it (if we insist on holding to the sequence of our own presentations, if we answer questions at much greater length in order to answer unasked questions), then we are merely imposing our views rather than listening.

There is an old (and unkind) joke about the dangers of imposing our own structure in questioning. It goes as follows:

In a murder trial, the defense attorney was cross-examining a pathologist. Here's what happened:

ATTORNEY: Before you signed the death certificate, had you taken the pulse?

CORONER: No.

ATTORNEY: Did you listen to the heart?

CORONER: No.

ATTORNEY: Did you check for breathing?

CORONER: No.

ATTORNEY: So, when you signed the death certificate, you weren't sure the man was dead, were you?

CORONER: Well, let me put it this way. The man's brain was sitting in a jar on my desk. But I guess it's possible he could be out there practicing law somewhere.

The basic sequence of listening is to let the speaker set the structure, and to be attuned to his or her structure until he or she is satisfied that we have grasped his or her meaning.

The Agenda-Setting Discussion.

Setting an agenda is very simple, is socially acceptable (i.e., no risk), and is very powerful. An agenda is a prestatement, a point of view in advance of a meeting, about how the meeting should be conducted and what should be addressed.

Asking, "What else should we discuss today?" or "What do we have to accomplish with today's meeting?" creates the opening for clients to tell us what is on their minds, and what their priorities are. Agenda setting, therefore, is a powerful formal tool for listening.

An agenda should never be presented without discussion. Instead, it should be used as a golden opportunity to have a brief, mutual discussion about how the meeting should be handled. The invitation to discuss an agenda, even if only for sixty seconds, sends a powerful signal at the outset that the meeting is being run for the mutual benefit of all present and is not the closely held property of one person or segment of the meeting.

An opportunity to use the agenda-setting tool arises at the start of almost any meeting, with two or two hundred people, between strangers or intimates, or whether on the first subject or the thirty-first. We should always begin the interaction by making the agenda itself a subject for discussion. "I thought it'd be useful if we talked mainly about ——— and ———, and then just a bit on —; how do you feel about that approach?"

We are talking here about both formal, written meeting agendas, and about verbal, small, even one-on-one implicit discussion agendas. If we behave as if one of us owns the agenda, has predetermined it, is wedded to it, and has a vested interest in maintaining it, then we have effectively created a "me versus you" dynamic. The forces that separate us have gained the upper hand.

If, on the other hand, through simple gestures and words, the agenda becomes shared, we have created and acted upon a powerful symbol for working together jointly. The client is made to feel *involved*.

What Good Listeners Do

What do good listeners do that makes them good listeners? They:

1. Probe for clarification
2. Listen for unvoiced emotions
3. Listen for the story
4. Summarize well
5. Empathize
6. Listen for what's different, not for what's familiar
7. Take it all seriously (they don't say, "You shouldn't worry about that")
8. Spot hidden assumptions
9. Let the client "get it out of his or her system"
10. Ask "How do you feel about that?"
11. Keep the client talking ("What else have you considered?")
12. Keep asking for more detail that helps them understand
13. Get rid of distractions while listening
14. Focus on hearing your version first
15. Let you tell your story your way
16. Stand in your shoes, at least while they're listening
17. Ask you how you think they might be of help
18. Ask what you've thought of before telling you what they've thought of
19. Look at (not stare at) the client as he or she speaks
20. Look for congruity (or incongruity) between what the client says and how he or she gestures and postures
21. Make it seem as if the client is the only thing that matters and that they have all the time in the world
22. Encourage by nodding head or giving a slight smile
23. Are aware of and control their body movement (no moving around, shaking legs, fiddling with a paper clip)

Here's what great listeners don't do. They *don't:*

1. Interrupt
2. Respond too soon

3. Match the client's points ("Oh, yes, I had something like that happen to me. It all started . . .")

4. Editorialize in midstream ("Well, that option's a nonstarter")

5. Jump to conclusions (much less judgments)

6. Ask closed-end questions for no reason

7. Give you their ideas before hearing yours

8. Judge you

9. Try to solve the problem too quickly

10. Take calls or interruptions in the course of a client meeting (it seems so obvious but watch how often it happens!)

12

Framing the Issue

FRAMING, THE THIRD STAGE in trust creation, is the act of crystalliz-
ing and encapsulating the client's complex issues (and emotions)
into a problem definition that, in an objective manner, provides
both insight and a fresh way of thinking about the problem. In
many advisory situations, an accurate problem statement is more
than halfway to the solution.

Of the five steps, framing is usually the most challenging, often
the most rewarding, and almost always the most difficult. This is
because framing is an inextricable combination of the rational and
the emotional, and must sometimes be conceived and articulated in
the middle of a conversation.

Framing involves identifying (and enunciating) the essence of
the issues at hand, usually something that is hidden, critical, fun-
damental, or all three. Identifying (and surfacing) the core "gut"
issue in a client situation will usually involve an emotional aspect,
in addition to the purely rational component.

Rational Framing

There are two kinds of framing: rational framing and emotional
framing. Generally, rational framing is far easier for advisors since
it is in our comfort zone. It is what we are trained to do.

Strategy consultants are especially prone to believing that their
clients are buying their brilliance and insight. Most firms stress
their ability to bring to the client the incisive application of intellect

in such a way as to create new perspectives, and hence open up new routes to shareholder value.

Lawyers, too, are expert at framing issues rationally. Such and such is an issue of tort law or constitutional law; it has this or that jurisdiction. Consider "the issue is, what did the President know, and when did he know it?" as a particularly successful example of legal, rational framing.

Rational framing is a key skill in the package of skills that advisors traditionally bring to bear. It is done in such deceptively simple ways as generating a list, drawing a diagram, or sketching out a process or approach. At root, all rational framing consists of distilling a complex set of issues down to a few critical variables.

Consider the use of a formal model (like our five-stage trust model), a method particularly beloved (and arguably overused) by management consultants. The reason for the prevalence of use of this technique is that the human mind has limitations on the amount of information it can process.

Amazing though humans are, we are considerably limited in the number of perspectives we can consider simultaneously. When we are confronted by too much complexity, we often fall into an endless cycle of frustration until we, or someone else, manages to simplify the problem statement. Then progress toward a solution can begin. Formal models do just that.

Rational framing looks so much like the "essence" of many professions that it's easy to forget it is only a *middle* step in a process of trust creation. The most brilliant, incisive insight will fall on completely deaf ears if the advisor has not yet earned the right to frame the issue by going through the necessary preceding steps of engaging and listening.

Advisors sometimes stress too much the need to create (and protect) proprietary framing methodologies or models. We think this concern is misplaced. There are relatively few great truths in life. The effectiveness of the advisor does not lie so much in the invention of the next (proprietary) paradigm as it does in finding the way to lead a particular client, with a particular problem, into seeing the *relevance* of an old (or new) paradigm.

Emotional Framing

Rational framing is a critical, even necessary, component of effective advising; but it is hardly sufficient. Frequently, advisory relationships (or discussions) get stuck in an emotional backwater. Ideas, conversation, and relationships stop flowing freely; they stagnate and begin to hamper effectiveness. Something must break the logjam that is inhibiting the discussion.

In such situations, the problem is not caused by (and cannot be solved by) a rational insight. What's causing the problem is predominantly an emotional or political issue.

David was once working with the executive committee of a professional firm on the topic of introducing new standards of performance and new accountabilities for all of the firm's partners. At one point in the meeting, they were discussing the (obvious?) managerial issue that something cannot be a standard if it is not enforced, or if the firm tolerates noncompliance.

On the surface, all seemed to be going well, and everyone seemed to be in agreement. However, David noticed some people shifting uncomfortably in their seats and a number of whispered side conversations going on around the table. "Something is going on here," he thought, but he was not entirely sure what.

He decided to try to address the issue. Calling on one of the whisperers, the following conversation ensued:

DAVID: Fred, I'm concerned that we are not getting all of the issues out on the table. Is there a complexity about doing this program at this firm that I'm not aware of?

FRED: Well, you seem to be saying that if one of our most powerful partners doesn't do this new thing, then someone will have to tackle him until he gets into compliance.

DAVID: That's exactly what we are all saying, I think. If exceptions are made to this standard for "big hitters," then it won't be credible as a firmwide standard to everyone else. Does anyone disagree with that?

The room fell silent. Finally, Fred spoke again.

FRED: But who's going to go and talk to this guy? I can't imagine telling our biggest rainmaker that he's got to change!

DAVID: I have an opinion, but before I give it, do you want to say who *you* think should have the responsibility?

FRED: I suppose it should be the managing partner.

At this point, Tom, the managing partner (who had been relatively silent,) jumped in.

TOM: Oh, I'll do it, but I need to know that the rest of the executive committee is solidly behind me. I can't do it, and won't do it if one or more of you break ranks. Do I have your full support? Will you all back me up if we go forward with this?

FRED: We'll back you up, Tom. But to be candid, you've never done such a thing before.

DAVID: Can I jump back in? None of you have done this before, and that's the point. We're here to discuss whether you *want* to do things differently from now on. You don't have to go through with this if you don't want to. But, as Fred has helped us understand, this is as much about having the courage and determination to see this through as it is about whether or not the plan is a good one. Shall we explore what it will really require from each of you?

It should be obvious from this dialogue that a hornet's nest of emotional and political issues had been raised. But what progress would this firm have made if they had not been raised?

Earlier in his career, David would not have had the courage to raise this topic openly. It would have been suppressed, and burst out only in stolen hallway conversations during coffee breaks.

However, we have all learned that solving clients' problems, in every profession, means helping the client (or the client's organization) solve not only the technical aspects of the problem but also the very real emotions that surround any kind of significant decision making.

Emotional framing is first and foremost about the courage to take a personal risk and surface hidden emotions. Naturally, this is not easy. But it can become an easier process than you think if you can remember that this is usually about framing the client's emotions (and not ours!). They're thinking about their situations and their reactions to them. So spending time focusing on how they make *us* feel is not really the issue. It makes things so much easier if you just have to deal with their emotions and not your own at the same time.

One of our friends, Joe, tells the story of a "lost sale" years ago. His client (a CEO) needed to do a major restructuring of his organization. The restructuring would involve asset sales, redeployments, and the laying-off of three to five thousand employees. Joe was not only the leading candidate to win the work, but at least for the moment, no competitors were being considered.

Discussions proceeded well. Toward the end of the second meeting with the client, everything seemed to be progressing as it should, and the meeting was heading toward a final handshake to close the deal. Then in an abrupt change of mood, the CEO leaned back in his chair and, shaking his head sadly, said, "Joe, what are we gonna do about all those people?" Joe was taken aback, and in the next instant, he made the *wrong* decision. He reverted to the upbeat mood of a moment before, slapped the CEO on the arm and said, "Hey, no problem, Bill. We'll line 'em all up with outplacement counselors, set 'em up in a separate building, they'll be out of here in no time. No problem."

But in the back of his mind he knew it wasn't right to make a joke of (and thereby cover up) the client's emotions. The meeting ended inconclusively. The next meeting got postponed, then never happened. In fact, the entire restructuring didn't happen for several more years, and, when it did (as Joe tells it), the layoffs totaled two to three times what they would have been originally.

In his mind, rightly or wrongly, Joe holds himself at least partly accountable for the incremental job losses, because he didn't have, in that moment, the ability to deal with the profound and personal sadness that the CEO was feeling. He thought that if he had had the courage and skill to help the CEO wrestle with the emotional complexity of the decision when it first arose, the pain and suffering felt by a lot of people (the client included) could have been avoided.

Naming and Claiming

A useful technique for emotional framing is a technique that we call naming and claiming. This phrase refers to the breakthrough that can come from speaking what hitherto may have been "unsayable," articulating something that was previously too uncomfortable to be stated.

Naming and claiming is characterized by three factors:

1. An acknowledgment of the difficulty of raising the issue

2. An acceptance of the responsibility for raising it

3. A direct statement of the issue itself

Many cultures have a phrase for such situations, where the embarrassment from the passage of time exceeds the original situation itself. We call it "the elephant in the parlor." This is a phrase for the "things that cannot be said," even though everyone knows them to be true. These situations can only be handled by emotional framing.

Using emotional framing is the equivalent of dynamiting a stream that has become clogged up to the point of dysfunctionality. There are echoes of emotional framing in psychotherapy and religion, in the bringing forth (through counseling or confession) of things that were previously left unsaid.

Ellen's Story

Ellen is a partner in an accounting firm who attended one of our programs. She was faced one day with the need to present some difficult news to her client, the controller.

As she began to deliver the bad news, she noticed that "the client's face was getting red, and his knuckles were getting white." We can all imagine the thousand and one emotions and thoughts that could be instantly conjured up by the active mind sitting in Ellen's chair in that moment: "How can I get out of here? There goes the account," and the like.

Yet Ellen took a different approach. She paused, took a deep breath, and said, "You look a little angry." And then she waited, silently, for the client to respond.

After a moment, the client shouted, "No, I'm not angry! Not at all!" He then added, "Well, I mean, not at you; I'm angry at our people. I mean, you shouldn't have to be the one to bring this news to me, it's embarrassing. I mean, I'm glad you've pointed it out. Yes, I'm angry, though not at you."

Ellen's reward for asking that question was clear and instant. She found out what the truth was, thereby freeing herself from the fears she had created internally. She allowed the client to blow off steam, to say just what it was that concerned him. She allowed the client to articulate the problem at hand, thus moving the conversation productively in the direction of a joint solution. And she created a further bond between herself and the client by being willing to reach outside her own fears and be of instant, personal service to the other person, her client.

The point here is not that Ellen had been in the right. The point is that Ellen chose consciously to focus not on her own mind (the thousand emotions and thoughts, each demanding its own version of talking faster and slicker) but on the mind of her client. She made a simple observation, one clearly about her client, not herself.

Had Ellen gone with her own fears, she probably would have delivered the bad news as quickly as possible and run for cover. If she had not asked the question, she would have left believing (incorrectly) that the client's anger was directed at her. Even if that had been the case, she would never have known if she had not asked the question (or made the observation).

Emotional framing is about taking risk. It requires some courage to say something that people are generally afraid to say. Ellen had the courage to treat the emotional signals (clenched fists, red face) that her client was sending as objective facts, rather than as judgments about her.

Framing and Blaming

Most initial attempts at framing, perhaps especially those made by clients, are laden with blame. "I can't get the marketing people to listen to me." "We need better training." "It won't work if the CEO isn't behind it." All these are typical problem statements that are not, from a trusted advisor's viewpoint, sufficiently free of blame to constitute useful framing statements.

Blame truly gets in the way of effectively framing the issue. In fact, it gets in the way of effective advising in general. An advisor spending any energy blaming a client (or almost anyone else) is wasting energy that could be focused on doing something useful for the client. Even in the rare cases where blame is "justified," it is useless at best. Blame is a defense mechanism protecting the ego of the one doing the blaming. As such, it is just another form of self-orientation.

By systematically telling the truth and eliminating blame from his or her repertoire, a trusted advisor can maneuver toward full ownership of a blame-free problem statement that can be acted upon, evaluated, and transcended.

How to Implement Emotional Framing

When we discuss examples such as those given above, we find that people can "get" every example we mention, but when describing their own "elephant" situations, they feel that "My situation is different. There's a lot at stake here; it's not play."

No, it's not play. That's why we all have to accept it as central to our roles as advisors. The essence of it is moving from a defensive or blaming attitude to an attitude of taking responsibility.

Being willing to move from blame to responsibility feels risky. Why should I give up the security of being able to blame someone else for difficult situations? Ironically, naming and claiming is a technique for accepting responsibility that actually reduces personal risk.

It's a technique that makes judicious use of caveats. The caveats are about how difficult it is to raise the issue in question and to take personal responsibility for the consequences of it being raised. Feel more risk? Add more caveats. Add as many as it takes, stringing them together up to the point at which you have just slightly over-compensated for the perceived risk of the issue you're about to frame. Choose from the following list of responsibility-taking caveats:

1. It's probably just me, but . . .
2. I must have been tuned out for a moment, I'm sorry, but . . .
3. I'm sure you covered this before, but . . .
4. I'm sorry to interrupt, but I just can't get this out of my head about . . .
5. You've probably thought of this already, but . . .

6. I wish I knew, but I just don't know how to handle this concern . . .

7. I realize you have a strong preference for XYZ, but . . .

8. I'm probably thinking about this all wrong, but . . .

9. I'm not sure if this is on point, but . . .

10. I may not have understood this right, but . . .

11. I don't know exactly how to say this, so I hope you'll help me, but . . .

12. I'm not sure if I'm being inappropriate in bringing this up, but . . .

13. I hope you'll forgive me for not knowing quite how to say this, but . . .

(Note that these are all phrases used by the TV character Lieutenant Columbo! See Chapter 17.)

Having posed enough responsibility-taking caveats, say the thing that must be said. Although emotional framing appears to be very risky, it offers enormous payoffs. Furthermore, it is the process of managing those risks by raising hidden topics, (emotional framing) that unleashes the payoffs. We cannot stress its importance enough.

13

Envisioning an Alternate Reality

Envisioning is the fourth stage in the process of trust creation, after engaging, listening, and framing.

As noted in Chapter 9, where we began to present the five-stage process, the role of joint envisioning in the trust-development process is to concretize a specific vision and choice among the many future states toward which the client might want to aim. In envisioning, the advisor and the client jointly imagine what the end result might look like, addressing the questions:

1. For what are we *really* aiming here?
2. What will it look like when we get there?
3. How will we know we are there?

Of the five stages, envisioning is the one most often neglected. Sales models, for example, may go straight from problem definition to action and solution. To some extent, focusing on benefits is parallel to what we call envisioning; but it is not the same thing.

The language of politics offers us some "sound-bite-sized" examples of envisioning, and hints at its value. Consider the New Deal, the New Frontier, the Great Society, or Martin Luther King's "I Have a Dream" speech.

These are all attempts to articulate, in a succinct way, the essence of something for which to aim, and something that actually *could be* attained with real effort. They have a tremendous impact on the building of energy and consensus by articulating a goal (and a way of thinking about that goal).

Envisioning is what we tried to do with you in Chapter 1, the Sneak Preview. We asked you to imagine what it would be like to be trusted by your clients, and whether you wanted those benefits. We also asked you to think about what your role would look like if you were a trusted advisor.

Successful envisioning in a business frees up people. It takes them far out of the technical, problem-solving, high-risk perspective with which they approach most problem solving, and into a new perspective. This new perspective is one that encourages freedom and creativity. Of all the steps in trust creation, it is the one that isn't absolutely necessary but can often add the greatest value.

United Research, a consulting firm that later became part of Gemini Consulting, made great use of this step in the 1980s and early 1990s. They employed a multistep sales process, including listening and diagnostic steps, but their key step was a large-scale exercise in envisioning.

They would interact with large numbers of people and ask them a series of leading questions. They would ask:

> "Could things be different around here? If so, could they be better? How? In what ways? What would things look like in this better future? What would have to change for that to happen? Where would the benefits show up?"

As people spent time on this envisioning step, they began to articulate in great detail just how things might look in a world where the major problem facing them had been solved, or the major opportunity in front of them had been attained. The idea rapidly took hold that real change could be accomplished and might be worth working for. Suddenly it was no longer abstract. It was real, and possible. And suddenly it was no longer scary. It was both energizing ("Let's go for it") and comforting ("We can do this").

This outcome is identical to what can happen in a two-person, relationship-building, trust-based conversation. By jointly focusing on a mutually attractive future, unencumbered by the problems of the present, barriers can be broken down and bridges can be built.

After successful listening and framing, there is a huge temptation to omit envisioning and to get to the next step (commitment and taking action), but it is a temptation worth resisting.

Grammar is a good guide here. Instead of using the words "why don't we?" at this stage, substitute the words "how would things be if . . ." Focus on descriptive sentences. Ask questions about things like benefits, end states, or outcomes.

An Illustration

Charlie had a client, Mark, who was extremely frustrated with a work situation. He had taken on an assignment, as a consultant, for the CEO of an existing client, despite an already heavy workload. While the assignment carried with it some risk of failure, the CEO assured Mark of his personal interest in the project and his intention to be fully available when necessary. Mark's primary contact was to be the chief operating officer.

A short time later, the chief operating officer experienced some severe personal difficulties and asked that Mark work with another executive. That person was goodwilled but often unknowledgeable and ineffective. After a time, Mark raised this issue with the CEO, but little changed as a result of this conversation.

As time passed, matters deteriorated; the CEO continued to be even less available, as did the chief operating officer, but there was no lessening of pressure to deliver results on the project. Predictably, Mark was upset and frustrated.

When Charlie first talked to him, Mark's way of framing the issue was:

> "The client is being very unfair to me: I took on some considerable risk based on his personal assurance of open access, but find that he is not delivering on his part of the bargain."

This instinctive way of framing the issue is perfectly understandable and natural, but nonetheless quite inappropriate. First, it is entirely about Mark, not the client. Second, it is loaded with speculative attributions of motive on the part of the client. Finally, it is judgmental.

Mark and Charlie worked together to reframe the issue by focusing more on the client, by removing the tone of blame, and by striving for objectivity rather than judgment. A step along the way sounded more like:

"I am upset because the client is not spending the time with me that I expected, thus jeopardizing the quality of the work."

However, this statement still suffers from self-focus, blame, and judgment. As they worked further, they agreed that a useful framing of the problem had to take into account the client's point of view. Not knowing his position, they had to hypothesize about it, as follows:

"Things have gotten busy. As a result, he hasn't been able to provide the time he had hoped to commit, which means he is in a position of having to do other than what he had promised. And I find myself in a position of possibly producing lower quality than I had promised. Neither of us is happy with the situation."

Based on this revised framing, Mark decided to try envisioning with his CEO client. He began the conversation as follows:

"Look, Albert, before we both jump to even more commitments we both might regret, can we take a minute and be sure we're in sync about what's at stake? What are we trying to accomplish? How will we know when we've got it right?"

Finally, they generated a picture of what might be, envisioning a different future, sounding something like:

"If we settled on a common view of where we're going, we'd be able to table an issue until we had time to talk about it, instead of worrying about what the delay meant. We'd know that a delay wasn't personal. We'd know that quality is always a variable, and that all decisions have impact. We'd raise issues more quickly. We wouldn't wait until crises came up. We wouldn't interpret events solely as personal failures or successes, but sometimes just as events. We'd have an agreed-upon formula, if not a schedule, that we both understood and could rely on. We wouldn't lose sleep worrying. We'd have confidence in each other."

Mark obtained the cooperation he needed to serve his client by getting him to envision the benefits of the future state.

Summary

It is very tempting to leave out the envisioning activity, and to slip into action language directly from framing. The client, in fact, is every bit as likely to say, after the problem has been defined, "Well, what can we do about this?" And the words "what can we do" are like a Pavlovian bell to many advisors: We feel we must respond because our self-image as technical masters is on the line.

How much better it is to be able to say, "Hold on, we'll get there, but let's first spend some time talking about where it is we want to go, and what it is we're really trying to achieve."

With a clear understanding of the destination, both parties to the conversation will have articulated just what is at stake, they will have signed up for the benefits, and they will both also have started the outline, the specifications, for what an eventual solution might look like. Having had such a conversation, they are now far better primed to talk about "what to do about it."

14

Commitment

By using the word "commitment," we do not refer to such activities as "closing the sale" or drawing up a contract for an engagement to proceed. Instead, we refer to the final stage of *trust building* (not selling) when the advisor ensures that the client understands what will be necessary to solve the problem and is willing to do what it takes to achieve the goals.

The dictionary gives two meanings for commitment: (1) an agreement or pledge to *do* something in the future, and (2) the state or an instance of *being* obligated or emotionally impelled.

The first is about action; the second is about an emotional state. It is the second that keeps us in the realm of the personal and emotional, which is what we think commitment should mean in the context of trust.

Without commitment, advice giving is merely the expression of opinions:

ADVISOR: You should do this!

CLIENT: Yeah, I should! Thanks! Good-bye!

If we have followed the trust-building process, we would now be at the stage where the problem has been framed to everyone's satisfaction, and what we are aiming to achieve (the vision) is also clear. What must now follow is a series of conversations on such topics as:

1. What's going to get in the way of getting this done?
2. What do we intend to do about it?
3. Who needs to be brought into the loop?
4. Who should do what part?
5. What information do we need?
6. When shall we check in?
7. What are the key deadlines?

This is not just about developing the advisor's work plan. It is about making sure the client understands all the down-and-dirty implementation details, all the difficulties he or she will face in pursuing the new path, what new behaviors it might require of the client.

Only when the he or she has been exposed to all of this will the client (and we) know whether or not commitment truly exists. There *is* a degree of self-protection in all of this: if our clients aren't committed to do what it takes to solve the problem, they won't benefit from our advice and we will have failed! (Even if everything we did was right!)

If we haven't been clear (up front) about the risks, barriers, and true requirements for success, then when pitfalls occur (ones that could or should have been foreseen), our client may feel we were less than open and less than professional at the start of the process.

Hence, the commitment process is saying something like:

"Let me test your resolve for committing to this course of action. Let's make sure we understand what will be required of each of us and where contingencies may arise. Let me play devil's advocate and try to convince you *not* to do all the things we just agreed to do."

Viewed this way, commitment is "buckling in for the ride!"

Trust is enhanced by the advisor's openness and candor. The advisor is providing an education, based on his or her experience, about something the client has perhaps never been through before.

Conversations that produce commitment are those that explore all aspects of what the proposed action will mean to the client. Examples might include "This will feel risky to you but it will pay off," or "This means you'll have to stretch into marketing areas you don't know," or "Cindy probably won't like this, and you will have to deal with that," and so on.

It can be very tempting to omit discussions of risks, uncertainties, and pitfalls at the beginning of an assignment, or worse, when we are still trying to win the assignment. A natural instinct is to project an air of "This can be done, no problem, leave it to us, we'll take care of everything!" This is often done in the mistaken notion that such phrases create trust by projecting self-confidence. Often, however, it can be interpreted as arrogance or secrecy ("What's he hiding?").

Clients usually commit for one of two reasons: Either they are feeling pain or energy around a topic; or they have been captivated by something new, different, and totally appealing.

Of these two reasons, what do you think the relative frequency of occurrence would be? Our guess is that the first reason, feeling pain or energy, drives client commitment about 80 percent of the time. Inspiration may be all well and good, but pain relief is a major driver. It is a prerequisite to anything else. This helps us at least consider whether we are offering inspiration or pain relief, and how we offer it, as well.

So, what do clients actually commit to? For many advisors the frequent answer to that question is "not enough." It often seems as if our clients will agree with us in principle, but fall down on practice. "You're right," they say. "We absolutely must do this, but right now there's so much going on that we simply don't have the capacity to tackle this now." We've all heard variations on this theme. There is not enough time, not enough budget, not enough organizational support.

Much of the time, clients commit to something slightly less than they could. It's largely a defense mechanism on their part. They need room to maneuver, just in the event something unexpected happens. Which it always does.

Nonetheless, we often find ourselves disappointed if our clients haven't taken advantage of all the wisdom we've got to offer. As trusted advisors, however, it's a gratifying statement that they have recognized the need to take action, and have actually committed to start going down a path with us.

The author and radio humorist Garrison Keillor often talks

about Powdermilk Biscuits, an imaginary product "that gives shy persons the courage to do what has to be done." When you consider all the advertisements we ignore, all the offers we dismiss, all the solicitations we refuse, it should be gratifying that our clients accept our guidance even part of the way.

Managing Expectations

A central part of building the commitment to act is carefully managing the client's expectations about what is and is not going to happen in solving the problem. When done well, this can build great trust by demonstrating that the advisor is knowledgeable about solving problems of this kind, and can anticipate in advance where the pitfalls and contingencies lie.

We must ensure that our clients gain a clear understanding of what they can and cannot reasonably expect from us, and of what both they and we must do. Expectations (on both sides) should be identified and understood up front.

Clients need to be made aware of every step we are proposing to take to reach their particular goal. Some clients may begin to take on too large a project or too many projects. We need to assess their commitment to, and capability of, doing what is necessary to achieve the goal they have in mind.

Some clients may even decide that they don't want to invest the time, energy, or resources necessary to make the project work. They may decide to scale back their expectations to something more realistic. The client should understand the specific results, outcome, or deliverables that our involvement is intended to produce, as well as the contingencies produced by their time and resource constraints.

To manage expectations well, we must:

1. Clearly articulate what we will do and won't do
2. Clearly articulate what the client will do and won't do
3. Define the boundaries of the analyses we will perform
4. Check with the client about areas that the client may not want us to get involved in, or any people the client does not want us to speak with

5. Identify precise working arrangements

6. Agree on methods and frequency of communicating

7. Decide who should get which reports

8. Decide how often a report should be delivered

9. Decide how any reports will get used

10. Decide what milestones and progress reviews are needed

11. Decide how success will be measured, both at the end and during the process

It may seem that these are low-level, picayune details. However, they are not. Through such detailed conversations, clients will gain the accurate impression that we are trying to serve them in the way they wish to be served. In addition, we will surface details of what they (and their people) will be expected to do, and avoid misunderstanding. Finally, we will ensure that they have a true understanding of precisely what they are agreeing to. That's commitment!

In building trust when managing expectations, we offer the following additional suggestions:

1. Always tell the exact truth about what you can (and can't) do, and when you can (and can't) deliver. Sometimes in an effort to get the work, we say yes to work that can only be completed (if at all) with great personal pain. It's not worth it. Repeat: It's not worth it. One more time, for emphasis: It's not worth it.

2. Start the project before you've been engaged.

3. Show your enthusiasm. It's a great client; it's work you like; it's work you wanted; they asked you to do it. What could be better?

4. Ask the questions that are troubling you earlier rather than later. Don't be afraid to reveal your thoughts early. It'll help the client see you're focusing on the tough issues right from the start.

We should also do as much homework about our clients as possible, a task made easier in a world of Internet Web pages and search engines. This will prove that we are at least trying to enter their world.

With existing clients, we could show them our full work plan and ask if they have any suggestions. This clearly demonstrates that we are trying to create a "we-not-me" orientation.

In some circumstances, we could offer to show clients the completed end product or work product of a similar assignment done for other clients, revised and disguised as necessary to protect the other clients' confidentiality.

We could offer ways to save them money on the assignment in advance, by showing alternate ways of solving the problem, giving a choice between the thorough version and the quick and dirty version!

We can be open about the challenges and difficulties of the work we're about to engage in. Apart from increasing our credibility and intimacy, it also shows a "we-not-me" attitude.

Resistance to Commitment

At the commitment stage, clients may resist taking actions that advance the issue at hand. Frequently, it is because the earlier steps in the trust process have not been adequately dealt with.

Charlie had a client with 700 retail stores. Every discussion about strategy and positioning seemed to start with one global vision statement, and seemed to end with someone pointing out that store #327 didn't fit the statement.

Charlie and his team suggested that perhaps there were not one or seven hundred store types, but suggested a fairly basic segmentation scheme by store type describing three types of stores. It was still hard to get commitment to even some noncontroversial implications. That is, until they came up with the idea of assigning each store to one of the three types and running a composite profit-and-loss statement. Suddenly they could quantify the results. All but a dozen got categorized, which means they had statistically isolated the historic disagreement about direction.

More important, the profit-and-loss statements were radically different. The most profitable group of stores had historically been the most shunned, because it had the highest shrinkage rates. The other two had radically different growth rates.

Suddenly commitment blossomed. Actions were taken in real estate and merchandising, all because a question had been framed and alternatives had been envisioned. Envisioning had moved from the abstract to the concrete.

When the client could see this, it became clear to them that it was in their best interest to commit to various actions (investment and divestment, refurbishment, merchandising) and to continue the strategic work together and with renewed trust.

In retrospect, it was clear that the client needed more envisioning. They had not been able to gain a clear idea of what this new segmentation scheme implied for their business. But by using a familiar descriptor, store income statements, they were able to envision (in familiar concrete terms) an alternative reality. With this in place, the commitment step was unblocked, and progress was made very quickly. The lesson is that when commitment appears to be in doubt, back up one (or even two) steps in the trust process.

There are other reasons clients resist commitment. Chief among these are fear and complacency. In such circumstances, what's an advisor to do? The advisor can do a service to the client in such times by naming and claiming the situation for what it is. If it is fear, then facing it begins by acknowledging it. If it is complacency, then it may be time for the advisor to expend some trust capital to heighten the felt tension to get the client "over the hump."

What kinds of actions serve to generate commitment? In our experience, the old combination of "who, what, when" is the most powerful guide. There is value to be added by connecting the (often pleasant but abstract) envisioning to the details of what actually might be. In this sense, commitment is about connecting the "as-is" state of affairs and the "to-be" situation.

Helping clients to commit can seem a little dull. It isn't. In fact, risk and emotions are likely to surface more here as they begin to realize the full scope of what they're about to undertake. Good commitment steps can greatly heighten enthusiasm and cement people's sense of belonging to an initiative.

Joint Commitment

Commitment in the context of the trust process differs from simple action planning in two respects; it is joint, and it is personal.

Consider a client-advisor relationship that works largely at the lower levels of trust, (i.e., the content expert level). At the end of a conversation, or a meeting, there might be a dialogue like this:

CLIENT (MYRA): All right, what we've said is that you will write up the outline for the program. Joe, you'll work on metrics, and I'll develop a presentation for the team. We should each have our pieces done for a review meeting on the twenty-eighth.

ADVISOR (ANDY): That sounds good. We have some great work on that topic; I'll send Joe some background material. Also, I'll have the outline done the day before.

Certainly this conversation covers the "who, what, when" criteria; it also shows the advisor reaching out to offer content and to exceed expectations. Yet, while it may be parallel, it isn't joint. And it isn't particularly personal. In this example, there is nothing about the commitment that makes the advisor's contribution differ from anyone else's. He or she could be replaced by another client person, or by another advisor.

What might the discussion sound like if it were trust based?

CLIENT (MYRA): All right, what we've said is that Andy will write up the outline for the program. Joe, you'll work on metrics, and I'll develop a presentation for the team. We should each have our pieces done for a review meeting on the twenty-eighth.

ADVISOR (ANDY): That sounds good, but I'd like to involve my colleague Judy in that program outline; she's got the banking perspective that complements my technology angle. OK if I run it by her first?

Joe, that metrics work is critical to your ABC division as well; may I let Bill Y., my client at ABC, know that you're working on it? I think he'd be very interested in what you've had to say about it.

Finally, Myra, remember what we agreed about your needing to delegate certain work and spend more time externally? Isn't this a case in point, an opportunity for you to change your habits?

In this case, the advisor adds value by placing the issue in the context of other work being done for the client, something that can be done by relatively few people. The commitment is two-sided, truly joint, and not just from a shared workload calculation.

The advisor is proposing a deepening of linkages on both the content side and the personal side. Relationships will be strengthened. The client's personal growth is seen as valid grounds for inclusion in this example of commitment. Embedded in the advisor's response is a further commitment of all parties not only to a particular set of action steps but also to a continued exploration of implications, and to the other individuals. Among other results, the advisor emerges from this conversation as playing a truly unique role, one that could not be performed by anyone else.

PART THREE

PUTTING TRUST
TO WORK

THE SECTION BEGINS with an exploration of the difficulties that we all have in applying the concepts and techniques discussed so far. This is followed by a related topic of how you apply the ideas presented thus far to different types of clients and different types of client situations.

We then take a brief detour in approach and look at a famous (albeit fictional) character's approach to dealing with people.

Next we explore building trust during four stages of the client-advisor relationship: getting hired, building trust on the current assignment, building trust away from the current assignment, and cross-selling.

Finally, we close with a list of practical tips.

15

What's So Hard About All This?

MOST, IF NOT ALL, of what we have had to say so far in this book is straightforward. Why, then, are skilled trusted advisors not more common? What's so hard about this?

There are many reasons people find it difficult to fulfil the trusted-advisor role. Here is a list of some of the more frequent comments we hear:

1. This is all too personally risky. The emotional stuff feels embarrassing, different, flaky.

2. It's not easy to stop worrying about yourself and focus on others instead.

3. Professional services firms often breed a culture of content expertise and mastery. (We're taught that content is all.)

4. We can't overcome our fears of looking ignorant, stupid, or uninformed, so we act assertively.

5. It's hard to shut up and listen before you solve the problem. We have a hard time rewiring our instincts or habits.

6. It takes a lot of courage to speak about the unspeakable. Some things you just don't say; they're too personal, too risky, or too unprofessional.

7. It comes too close to the line of invading the private.

8. This approach discounts too heavily the value of good content or expertise.

9. It all sounds too moralistic.

10. This process sounds s-l-o-w! My budget won't allow for this!

11. My client wants me to focus on the work at hand; he or she doesn't want to see me about anything else.

12. It's risky to take a position on an issue until I'm absolutely sure.

13. I took a position, and now I'm stuck with it. To change my view would destroy my credibility!

14. It's hard to be this humble!

Let's examine each of these in turn.

1. This is all too personally risky. The emotional stuff feels embarrassing, different, flaky.

That's right. It *is* risky, and if we don't do it with careful balance, it will come off as flaky, and we will feel embarrassed. So careful balance is the key. It means awareness, focus, and practice. The fact that it doesn't get done often is an opportunity, not a problem. It's a chance to distinguish ourselves. Risk is the essence of creating intimacy.

2. It's not easy to stop worrying about yourself and focus on others instead.

Right again. For most of us, "us" is our favorite subject. But we get so much better at being ourselves if we focus on what other people are worrying about. It helps us find ourselves. Remember the quote from Ralph Waldo Emerson: *"Who you are shouts so loud I cannot hear what you say."*

New ways of thinking and behaving can be learned, but we have to practice them.

3. Professional services firms often breed a culture of content expertise and mastery. (We're taught that content is all.)

The fact that we're taught it is absolutely no guarantee that it's right, just that it's common. The statement is accurate, but incomplete. Many professional firm cultures do breed a cult of exclusive focus on content mastery. After all, it's so measurable, so quantifiable.

But it's probably also fair to say that leading professional services firms have made (or are attempting to make) the adjustment to an approach that recognizes just *how little* content mastery matters if the client does not trust us. We would venture to say that truly *great* professional services firms (and those of the future) haven't just made the adjustment to that approach; they are (or will be) built on it.

4. We can't overcome our fears of looking ignorant, stupid, or uninformed, so we act assertively.

Oh, yes we can. It's just that it's hard or we're out of practice, or we don't realize that we look even *more* ignorant, stupid, or uninformed if we let pure assertiveness take over.

These fears are a normal human response, like fight or flight. That doesn't mean we can't overcome them. What also makes us human is our ability to recognize our feelings for what they are and to transcend them. The essence of "emotional intelligence" is the ability to recognize and interpret emotions in ourselves and in others and to act on that interpretation rather than be blindly driven by the pure emotions themselves.

5. It's hard to shut up and listen before you solve the problem. We have a hard time rewiring our instincts or habits.

It is indeed hard to shut up and listen. Those instincts and habits are wired deeply. But they can be and are changed every day by many people. The first step is to recognize them for what they are, just ingrained habits. The three of us still feel we haven't gotten it right personally. We get overexcited when we think we know the answer to a client's question, and jump in with an answer before the client has even finished describing the situation. We may think we are proving our value by providing a speedy answer, but it is more than possible that the client has a negative reaction and thinks we are not listening and are too eager to show off.

Rob is trying the following technique: He's learning to control himself by keeping a pen in his right hand (he's left-handed) and forcing himself to at least wait long enough to switch his pen to the opposite hand. We all have to find habit-breaking devices (simple as they may be) that will work for us. Otherwise we're stuck in the old behaviors.

6. It takes a lot of courage to speak about the unspeakable. Some things you just don't say; they're too personal, too risky, or too unprofessional.

Right again. It does take courage. One thing that helps, and gives us courage, is the realization that very often, the alternative (i.e., not speaking up) can be worse. It means a lost opportunity to help someone who could actually benefit from it. Without risk, there is a guarantee of only a limited intimacy, and hence to trust. In our experience, advisors vastly overrate the risk of taking an action, and underrate the risk of not taking an action.

7. It comes too close to the line of invading the private.

If we have sincere respect for the other person, the words that convey it will probably come. Most people welcome interventions made with respect. When they don't welcome it, they don't return respect with indignation, but with a simple "No, thank you."

Most advisors, when they feel that something comes "too close" to invading the private, are actually not referring to how the other person will feel, but are focused on their own worries about how they will feel in response to the other person's response.

If we invade the private, we *are* too close to the line. It's why nam-ing and claiming, and gentle phrasing, and giving people an "out" are so valuable.

8. This approach discounts too heavily the value of good content or expertise.

Discounting? No way! This approach actually *enables* good content and expertise to be effective. If we don't have an adequate level of trust, no content and expertise will ever get through.

9. It all sounds too moralistic.

It would be moralistic if it were judgmental, and if we were critical of others who fail to follow this approach. We're not. We are not moral-ists, but we do know that this approach *works*. It can make you suc-cessful in ways that would otherwise not occur.

Evaluate it purely in pragmatic terms, based on your own observa-tions. Does trust succeed as a strategy? Do people buy to a great extent on the basis of trust and relationships? Do people respond positively or negatively to an outreach on the part of another person? Ask your-self if it works. Let your own experience be your guide.

10. This process sounds s-l-o-w! My budget won't allow for this!

This makes two false assumptions. First, it assumes that clients won't pay for counseling time. The real-world truth, is that since the counseling is done with them, in their presence, they more readily per-ceive the value of counseling (and will pay for it) than they can per-ceive the value of what advisors do back in their own offices.

Second, the concern assumes that time spent advising a client must be recouped on the current assignment, when the truth is that, done well, effective counseling (reimbursed or not) can be the most effective means of generating future revenues that exists. Which would you rather do? Be someone's counselor, or write proposals?

11. My client wants me to focus on the work at hand; he (or she) doesn't want to see me about anything else.

Unless and until you earn the right to do otherwise, this may well continue. It's worth an attempt every now and then. You can do clients a service by stating to them (very clearly, very directly, one time) that you perceive them as wanting you to focus on the work at hand, and that they don't want to see you about anything else. Ask to confirm this observation, because you intend to deliver on it and want to make sure that you've got it right.

Then listen closely to the client's answer and be prepared to deliver based upon it. If, at a certain point, you feel the situation will simply never change, then thank heavens you now have a clear sign that your investment in becoming a trusted advisor to a client will be better made elsewhere.

12. It's risky to take a position on an issue until I'm absolutely sure

It's risky to take a *hard-wired* position on an issue until you're absolutely sure. If you take a preliminary position with your client, make sure that it is just that, and that he or she acknowledges it as such. Then you can actually look pretty good most of the time, and pretty thoughtful all of the time.

There are sins of omission and sins of commission. Not taking a position sacrifices an enormous range of options for helping a client. It diminishes the possibility of framing hypotheses, brainstorming, stimulating conversation, and gaining the client's insight by involving them in evolving thinking. For the sake of an inward fear (read self-orientation), this so-called risk aversion surrenders many positives. It isn't risky to do this; it's unprofessional *not* to do it.

13. I took a position, and now I'm stuck with it. To change my view would destroy my credibility!

Our credibility is far more at stake if we are seen to be sticking to an incorrect view in the face of new data or thinking, than it is to admit we were wrong. Admitting we were wrong is admitting we are imperfect (i.e., human). Not to admit so is to claim we're omnipotent. To cling to a wrong idea for the sake of "credibility" is also the height of self-orientation, because it's all about us, and not at all about the facts or the client.

14. It's hard to be this humble!

Humility is not weakness. Serving others does not require us to be servile. Ego strength means not having to have our egos stroked continuously. Recognizing and respecting the strength in others does not diminish our respect or strength.

In summary, we believe that the risks of failure in trying to build trust are overrated, as long as people are self-aware enough to avoid being obnoxious. We've never heard of anyone who actually tried to build trust and failed.

Why We All Rush to Action Too Soon

There is one mistake made more commonly than all the others combined, which is simply jumping ahead in the trust process to driving for action before completing the other steps.

Imagine yourself as a systems consultant. You are meeting a potential client from a new part of an organization you already know reasonably well. After some pleasantries, the potential client begins to tell you about some performance problems in his system.

You nod your head vigorously, interjecting "uh-huh" know-ingly at all the right hardware and software references. You drop in a few "Yes, they have that same problem over at [the part of the or-ganization you know really well]." After a while, you are pretty sure that what you suspected all along is in fact the case; they have an architecture design issue. You ask the one killer question to make sure, and, voila! You get the answer you expected!

"Listen," you say, "what if we reconfigured some basic archi-tectural features. It wouldn't have to take long (we have a propri-etary process for doing it, called IMEX; I'll leave you a brochure) and it'll not only solve the performance problems you're having, it'll make your users love you."

And then, to your chagrin, the client backs off. Why? Because even if your answer is absolutely, completely, 100 percent correct, the client will not buy it (in fact will resist buying it) until and un-less you earn the right to even discuss a problem statement. You have not *earned that right*.

The interesting point is not *that* we jump too soon to commit-ment and action, but *why* we do so. There are four reasons why ad-visors jump to action too soon:

1. The human tendency to focus on ourselves
2. The belief that we're selling only content
3. The desire for tangibility
4. The search for validation.

The Tendency to Focus on Ourselves

So much of our time is spent focusing on ourselves, and so much of other people's time is spent focusing on themselves, that it is a rare and surprising event whenever someone breaks the veil. Sincere in-terest in another person comes across strikingly simply because it is unusual.

A *New York Times* survey showed the same result. Sixty percent of Americans said that you couldn't trust most people, but only 20 percent said they couldn't trust most of the people they knew. In other words, the more we know someone, the more likely we are to assume that we can trust him or her.

In one extensive executive education program, we asked one

question in every session and never once received a different an-swer. The question was, "Who operates at a higher level of trust-worthiness: you or your colleagues?" The answer, time and again, was "me." Specifically, some 800 participants rated 15 percent of their colleagues at the lowest level of trustworthiness. Yet only one of the 800 rated themselves as being at that bottom level.

We are not completely sure what this finding means. It may mean people are egocentric, or that they have a healthy respect for themselves, or that they are hopelessly self-centered. It clearly *does* mean that people trust what they know.

We all rate our own intentions higher than those of other people. In professional services (a business in which there is *nothing else but* human beings), this observation takes on critical business importance.

Action is the one step that feels as if it is mostly about us as ad-visors. It is about answers, and it feeds our desire to show that we are the answer experts. We are the ones suggesting action, and ac-tion usually consists of something we know how to do.

The Belief That We're Selling Only Content

A lawyer friend of ours (one of the top in his field) told us he be-lieved that the key to success in the law is to be one of the top two or three content experts in your city in your field. By that definition, there are probably fewer than 100 successful lawyers in the entire city of New York. Without trying to take a position on the absolute levels of importance of relationships and content, this feels restric-tive to us.

It's harder now for advisors to stay current. For physicians, it is literally a physical impossibility to keep up with research papers. For lawyers, it is the same. For management consultants, the sky is the limit in terms of how well read one would like to be. For ac-countants, the tax code is massive enough to defy any one individ-ual's attempt to master it. With all this effort, it is tempting to believe that when we have mastered the content, we have done enough.

Clients add fuel to this fire because they espouse the belief (at their conscious level, that is) that content is king. They will charac-terize their lawyers, accountants, and consultants as content experts. When they compliment you, it is likely to be about your technical mastery.

While this is misleading, it is a strongly held belief, one that causes advisors to instinctively jump ahead in the trust-development process to what looks like content—the step that says "let's get to action"!

The Desire for Tangibility

In the professions, problem solving is highly valued. Problem solvers, like nature, somehow abhor a vacuum. They are very uncomfortable with the uncertainty inherent in the early parts of the trust-development process. They seek to fill silences with hypotheses, and they seek to fill hypothesis gaps with data questions.

It's therefore not surprising that for many, a hint of ambiguity or uncertainty is uncomfortable. Advisors are, in effect, trained not to ask open-ended questions, but rather to ask closed-ended ones that reinforce hypotheses and showcase brilliance. We are often explicitly trained to control meetings, not to risk them being hijacked by clients.

In this ambiguous world, it is not surprising that there is respite when one finally gets down to action steps: who'll do what, with what resources, by when, in what order, costing how much, to what kinds of specifications, and so forth. Action is tangible, and the need for it is deeply built into many professionals' psyches.

The Search for Validation

Finally, professionals live in a paradoxical world, and unconsciously live out that tension. Consider these common sources of confusion for the typical professional:

- We must master huge levels of concrete detail, yet our "product" is rarely tangible.

- We often work in firms that have mission statements espousing the value that the firm is ranked ahead of the individual, but we are also frequently told that most clients buy individuals, not firms.

- Many professional service firms talk about the importance of people, yet have high turnover rates. They simultaneously talk about the need to "prune" for quality (fire), and the need to "attract and retain the best" (hire).

- Professionals who leave and then return to their firms all cite "the people" as the primary competitive attribute of their firm, no matter which firm it is. Yet attention to skills in dealing with people is often neglected.

- Most professionals don't like to be seen as "selling," even though they are supposed to "develop business" by mid-career, or even earlier.

- Psychologically, in our experience, many professionals are both slightly insecure and slightly egocentric.

Amid this confusion, there is a tremendous desire for positive feedback from the client, because it is the client who trumps all at the end of the day. Feedback comes largely from the client's reaction to our action activities. It is only then that the normal, slightly nervous professional can be really, really sure that everything is OK. It is at that point that commitments are made, financial and otherwise. Only then does the professional get the chance to apply what he or she was trained to do: apply technical skills. Until then, everything feels uncertain.

These tendencies are virtually hard-wired in us. In our executive education work, we find some slight amusement in telling people right before a role-play of the trust process that the error they will most likely commit is that of jumping to problem solving and action. They then proceed, almost inevitably, to prove the point.

Without conscious self-control and practice in controlling our instincts, new habits do not develop. Learning to interact with other people in new ways is not something that can be absorbed instantaneously. Many of us have a lifetime of bad habits to break.

There are strong instincts working against the natural development of trusted relationships in business, and we all need conscious self-discipline (and self-awareness) in modifying our instinctive approaches.

Risk

Rebecca, a management consultant, told us of a client relationship from her past. The project had gone well, and she had enjoyed the relationship, but had not tried to maintain it after the project was over. A year later, the client called Rebecca and said, with a touch of hurt in the tone of voice, "How come you never called? I thought we had a good relationship, and I could have used your help several times." Rebecca later explained to us the reason she had not maintained the contact: "I thought it was too risky. It might have been perceived as presumptuous. I figured, if she needed me, she'd call." What a shame; for all involved!

The number one reason (on our list, anyway) that people don't "do this trust stuff" is usually expressed as: "Well, I wouldn't do that, it's just too risky." The word *risk* comes up continually. Let's examine just what people mean by this.

First of all, what kinds of things do people find "risky?" Nearly everything we have listed are ways to increase trust: staking out a point of view, naming and claiming, reflective listening, observing an emotional fact, working the trust process rather than jumping to action. The very steps we recommend are those most commonly cited as being infeasible, because they are too risky!

This doesn't mean we are right or wrong. It simply means that trust-enhancing steps *do* carry some connotation of risk. Risk isn't antithetical to trust; risk is part and parcel of trust. So when people say, "That won't increase trust, it's too risky," we say, "Taking a risk is *precisely* how you build trust."

Second, what we hear expressed as business risk turns out to be, on close examination, personal risk. We hear generally two kinds of risk-averse comments: perceived risk to credibility, and perceived risk to intimacy. These are analyzed in Figure 15-1.

The perceived risk about credibility is based on a misconception about what it means to be a professional. Too many service professionals (and clients, if you ask them directly) labor under several misapprehensions about professionalism. They believe that to be professional means:

1. You must have the answers.
2. You must be quiet if you don't know the answer (and to find another professional with the requisite expertise as quickly as possible).
3. You keep the total knowledge base somewhat under wraps.
4. You must (generally) keep any gaps in your knowledge base hidden from the client.

Fig. 15.1. Reasons for Perceived Risk

Perceived Risk to Credibility:	"You Can't"	"Because the Client Wants"
	Hypothesize	An answer
	Say you don't know	Confidence
	Focus on the problem statement	Expertise
Perceived Risk to Intimacy:	**"You Can't"**	**"Because the Client Wants"**
	Stay with listening too long before moving to action	Action
	Get too personal	A "professional" relationship
	Talk about emotions	Just the facts
	Go off-agenda	Progress
	Point out difficult situations	To not be embarrassed

With this view of professionalism, no wonder it appears risky to openly admit ignorance, to suggest that further refinement of the problem statement might be in order, or to suggest that a series of hypotheses or points of view might actually advance the cause rather than signal incompetence.

The sense of credibility risk thus hinges on a narrow sense of professionalism, which we called exclusive rather than inclusive professionalism.

The perceived risk of intimacy comes from the (mistaken) idea that clients do not want to broaden the agenda beyond the purely rational. Clients themselves will hardly volunteer the idea that they want a deeper, more intimate relationship with their service providers. But the same clients will be the first to say that a primary buying criterion is the *understanding* their provider has of their specific situation (not situations like this in general).

Most research on buying suggests unambiguously that buying is a highly emotional process. This is perhaps particularly true for large-ticket, highly differentiated, complex purchases like professional services. In such an environment, both sides find it easy to kid themselves that logic must prevail and that the client does not want intimacy. But buying is an emotional act. Virtually always.

There are two kinds of risks: The risk of doing a wrong thing, and the risk of not doing a right thing. Most business people are paralyzed by the fear of the first kind of risk, often to the extent of unintentionally committing the second kind, which is more insidious and harmful than simply doing the wrong thing. To do a wrong thing is an understandable mistake, one we can learn from and, we would hope, be forgiven for. But to not do a right thing typically involves willful ignorance (or arrogance) over an extended period of time, and indicates lack of personal courage.

Even these two aspects of risk, however, don't explain everything. How do we explain Rebecca, who assumed that her client didn't care much about continued contact? There is another level of beliefs or feelings at work, some form of fear that the advisor feels.

Fear of what? Here we can generate quite a list. It would include fear of:

1. Not having the answer
2. Not being able to get the right answer quickly
3. Having the wrong answer
4. Committing some social faux pas
5. Looking confused
6. Not knowing how to respond
7. Having missed some information
8. Revealing some ignorance
9. Misdiagnosing

People in the service professions are a bit hard on themselves. Perhaps this is the sign of the overachiever. Perhaps it comes from working in a business where there is no practical upper limit to quality. Being overachievers cursed with an ability to envision a great number of ways to fall short, it makes sense that our worst nightmares tend to center on these fears. However, if our fears dominate our behavior, we will never take a risk and will accomplish much less.

Finally, it may be that the professions are havens of rationality for those less comfortable with a more direct, emotional approach to life. Good social skills and an excellent mind, in the professions, can generally compensate for a very large degree of emotional avoidance. Combined with an ethos that worships the mind, it is not surprising that some advisors feel that working on the intimacy part of the trust equation is risky.

The good news is that an attempt to take a personal risk is far more often than not returned by the other party, thus increasing intimacy. The only sure way not to lose the game is never to play the game at all. After all, as the Sicilian proverb says, *"Chi gioca solo non perde mai,"* or "If one plays alone, one never loses."

Managing Your Own Emotions

How much of being a successful trust-based advisor comes down to managing one's own emotions? Probably quite a lot.

Consider a simple example to which we can probably all relate. Imagine yourself in the early stages of fact finding with a client, in a meeting with several other people, with a number of unfamiliar concepts floating around. Someone mentions the "XP-27 situation," and many of the others laugh knowingly. You don't know what it's about. Do you stop and ask? Or do you let the meeting continue, figuring that perhaps you missed something from the pre-read materials, and that you'll pick up the issue in context as the meeting goes along? (After all, you have probably done pretty well for yourself so far in your career by picking things up from their context.)

Suppose you do the latter. Then suppose that a few minutes later, another similar moment arises, where someone refers to the RB-5, and someone else says, "Yes, and if it's like that, it'll make the XP-27 look like small beer!" Everyone laughs and nods vigorously. Except you, of course, because you haven't a clue what anyone is talking about. Meanwhile, the conversation rapidly turns to other topics.

Now you have a slightly bigger problem. If you stop the conversation to ask what it all means, you run the original risk of looking unstudied or out of it. You also run the risk of looking like you tried to outrun the risk in the first place, by not asking about the XP-27 when it first came up. And, as you ponder this latest development, your attention is nowhere near being focused on the conversation, thus setting you up even more for further confusions yet to come.

A trivial example, to be sure. But most of us know how to deal with this. We have all had to say things like, "I'm probably the only one who didn't do our reading last night, but . . ." or "At the risk of sounding silly, could someone help me understand . . ." So, why don't we do this more often?

The truth is that the higher the stakes, the harder it is to take those simple, little, self-correcting steps. Our emotions overrule what our heads tell us is the wisest thing to do.

Our own emotional needs (such as ego fulfillment) often dominate our reactions, rather than a calm, cool reflection along the lines of "What am I trying to achieve at this stage and what's the best way for me to get there? What should I say now, and how should I say it?"

A trusted advisor is above all someone who is capable of totally and completely devoting himself, his caring, and his attention to the client. The biggest obstacle to doing that is the tendency to devote our caring and attention to ourselves. And the root reason for that is self-centered fear; fear of losing what we have or not getting what *we* want.

Emotions and desires we must learn to control include:

1. Wanting (needing?) to take credit for an idea
2. Wanting to fill blank airtime with content
3. Playing to our own insecurity by feeling we have to get all our credentials out there
4. Wanting to put a cap on the problem so we can solve it later, without the pressure
5. Wanting to hedge our answers in case we're wrong
6. Wanting (too soon) to relate our own version of the client's story or problem

16
Differing Client Types

ONE OF THE DANGERS of writing, speaking, and teaching on the topic of trust building is the tendency to overgeneralize about clients and assume they are all alike. It's tempting, but it's dangerous and it's wrong. All of our work (and probably yours, too) shows just how different clients can be. In that vein, it's valuable to think about how to recognize and deal with the varying types of clients that one encounters.

We offer a collection of guiding principles, provided in order to help you think through how best to interact with clients of varying types.

1. Work in advance on what is different about this client, and what might be different about you in this situation.

Think about how this client compares to others where you have been at your most successful and at your least successful. Take at least one lesson from each of those with you *every* time you visit a client.

Rob remembers attending the offsite meeting of a fast-growing consulting firm. After all, one of the firm's founding partners had invited him, hoping that Rob would offer some of his wisdom on delivering consulting advice at the firm's meeting. Rob happily prepared his ninety-minute session, added a catchy title (something along the lines of "Even Streisand Gets Stage Fright, and Even Mick Jagger Has to Rehearse"), and went in with spirits high.

Unfortunately, the partner who had invited Rob had neglected to tell his two cofounders the reasons behind the invitation, and (equally unfortunately) had neglected to brief Rob. Rob had not been told that there was substantial internal disagreement on precisely how this firm should position itself in front of clients, precisely what its consulting end-product should look like, and precisely how it would deliver its messages. In addition, the inviting partner made only the most perfunctory of introductions at the start of the session, and then left the room.

The two remaining founding partners took this opportunity to interrupt the session barely five minutes after it had started. One of them began (quite belligerently) to challenge the entire premise for the session itself, thereby opening a debate inside the meeting room that lasted for the better part of an hour.

Needless to say, Rob's session on delivering advice to clients never got off the ground. Rob still remembers the shell-shocked feeling as it ended. One of the firm's less senior partners walked past him, shrugged his shoulders and said, "Nice try."

This story serves as a reminder to make sure that there is a *complete* understanding of what you're supposed to be doing for the client before you walk in to a meeting.

David had a similar experience with an ongoing client. He was hired to facilitate this firm's annual retreat for the third year in a row. Since he had extensive experience with this firm, he assumed that he knew all he needed to know. Alas, the meeting was a disaster because it emerged that the group was distinctly divided this year, and no one had briefed David on the new circumstances.

Naturally, it was David's instinct to protect his own ego and say it was the client's fault, because the client should have briefed him. However, David quickly came to realize what should have been the obvious lesson: It was *his* professional obligation to seek out such things beforehand. As we mentioned in our discussion on emotional framing, trusted advisors must avoid assigning blame and must assume responsibility for the success or failure of the process.

What David should have done, even at the risk of being seen as pushy, is to have asked his primary contact a series of delicate questions:

- Are there any topics I should avoid because they are too delicate to discuss in a large forum?
- Are there any topics on which the views of your colleagues are significantly divided?

- Where are we likely to encounter the most resistance?
- Do you have any initiatives already going on that might interact with the discussion of this one?

The trusted advisor, to be effective, must ask questions of this sort in advance.

2. As you look at a client, force yourself to ask three questions:

- What is the client's prevailing personal motivation?
- What is their personality?
- How does the state of their organization affect their worldview?

Having answered these questions, force yourself to address the question, "How do I adapt my style and approach to deal with this person as he or she likes to be dealt with?"

3. When thinking about a client's prevailing personal motivation, which of the following comes first?

- the need to excel?
- the need to take action and achieve results?
- the need to understand and analyze before deciding?
- the need to drive consensus?

Depending on which comes first (or how they rank overall), you at least have the chance to tailor your conversation to a specific outcome (excellence, action, analysis, or organizational consensus).

When thinking about a client's personality, how do you match? While every kettle may have a cover, one size doesn't fit all. Some people are reflective; others enjoy faster-moving interactions. In other situations, the reverse is true. Sometimes we have a colleague we can play off of, and sometimes we need to make adjustments.

It is said that good acting is not lying, but focusing on the one aspect of your own personality or character that is needed for the role, and then suppressing the other aspects of your own personality. This is good advice. Don't fake it, lie, or misrepresent, but find that part of you that can empathize in this situation.

Even if we match the client's prevailing personal motivation as well as their personality, and even if we've got the timing right, there's still one more issue that can trip advisors up. That has to do with taking the measure of the organization. People who have been optimists in one organization can change companies and get caught in an entirely different wind. We have all seen people undergo what seems a drastic personality change merely by changing roles.

4. Figure out why you might truly like this client as a person.

Try to find something that is special, fun, meaningful, or engaging about this person that you can relate to. You don't have to like everything about your client, but if you can find something to focus on, you will find it easier to behave appropriately.

If nothing comes to mind easily, or if nothing about them reminds you of something you like (or someone you like), that's a very big hint that this is probably not the best type of client for you, and no amount of adjusting one's personality will help.

This is not categorizing, or stereotyping, or suggesting that each client must fit into a particular box. Instead, it helps us focus on the most important client types of all: the ones with whom we are most likely to connect, to enjoy, and to whom we can be trusted advisors.

5. Use the trust equation.

Another approach to trying to figure out how to deal with clients of different types is to note their differences with respect to how they react to the key models of trust development.

Not every potential client will place the same weight on each factor of the trust equation. The first broad cut is how much time or emphasis or experience the individual places on the first two components, credibility and reliability. For many clients, credibility and reliability will be "entry factors" at early stages of a trust interaction. They will deal with intimacy and self-orientation only after having been satisfied about credibility and reliability.

For other clients, this initial phase will last much longer. It may be that their way of assessing intimacy and self-orientation is to "buy time" by talking about more conventional issues. It may be that their reason for focus on credibility and reliability is that they feel they "should" focus on the more objective features first; or it could be simply that they are more comfortable in the objective realm. The reasons don't matter.

Clients who are comfortable with the intimacy and self-orientation factors will signal this early. Clients who are comfortable with the credibility and reliability factors may need to be led to the intimacy and self-orientation factors. Yet while they may not lead the way, it doesn't mean they don't need to go there; it just means you need to do the leading.

What kinds of people are focused on each of the factors? We suggest you ask yourself the following questions about your particular clients; you probably know the answers for each individual. And, after all, that is what matters.

- How highly does my client value me for my objective, unbiased, clear opinions, considering me to be a haven of credibility?
- How highly does my client value me for my track record with him, my integrity in doing what I said I'd do?
- How highly does my client value the fact that he can talk to me about just about anything, without fear of embarrassment or breach of confidentiality?
- How highly does my client value the fact that I am on his side, that I am in this for him or her?

There are individual differences that also cut across situations, and about which generalizations can be made. There are some clients who place a very high value on being understood. Such people may grant you considerable leeway in moving quickly through the remaining steps of the process.

There are others who place disproportionate emphasis on listening, not out of hunger, but rather out of preference. These are typically people who themselves are adept at rich communication. If you find such people, get down to real issues quickly. Not only can you do so with low risk, but they will appreciate you for it.

Highly rational people place disproportionate emphasis on framing, whether it is rational or emotional. They use flip charts and (erasable) markers, the language of hypotheses and points of view, and verbal techniques that encourage bold thinking.

Emotional framing is appropriate where people are feeling conflicted, frustrated, wildly happy, embarrassed, or carefree. It can be done directly, but it should often be done in private, with care. While a few people are chronically subject to emotional states that have business impacts and require framing, most people just *occasionally* find themselves in such situations. So the appropriate approach is determined not just by the person, but by the situation the person is currently in.

The people for whom structured envisioning is most useful are those who tend to be deductive, critical, structured, highly rational, and skeptical, as well as those who are adept at blue-sky thinking and are highly creative types.

For the first type, this is partly because envisioning firms up benefits, thus addressing the skeptics and the critics. It is also because envisioning is an exercise that can leverage the talents of deductive and structured thinking, if it is set up right. Finally, it appeals to the rational because it strikes people as a "sensible" way to go about examining what might in other settings be perceived as "soft."

For the second type, envisioning works because it encourages a free-form, highly creative use of the imagination.

We discourage the instincts of clients who are inclined to jump to action steps in the trust process. This is because action, as discussed before, is better viewed as a natural outcome of the earlier steps in the process.

Some Difficult Client Types, and How to Respond

Having made quite a point of how clients differ, and how important it is that we focus on their differences, we will now take the risk of suggesting several broad patterns or types of behaviors we have observed in clients. These are archetypes or constructs built up to help us focus on what are admittedly always more complicated personalities.

Type 1. The "Just the Facts, Ma'am" Client

Client: "Just give me the facts. Answer when asked. Don't sell me. Why is the price so damn high? I'm the boss here."

Response (clarify and confirm): Don't get fooled by the content of what this client is saying. This is a plea to be understood, like any other; for some, it is even masking a fear of being wrong or wronged. The trick is to speak in the client's language, not yours. Use clarifying and confirming statements. Affirm his values; then try to behave that way, every once in awhile checking again.

Answer: "OK, I get it. You don't want to mess around with niceties. You want to get straight to the point. You don't want to waste time. You want me to have content every time we talk. That's the kind of person you are. Have I got it?"

Type 2. The "I'll Get Back to You" Client

Client: "That sounds fine, but I don't want to make any promises here. I don't want to get anyone's hopes up. I have to go back and think about it and talk about it with the boss. I'll speak with you later."

Response (anticipate): This is typically a client who is nervous about making judgments, much less commitments, on the spot. They are conservative, concerned about being wrong, and prefer to have time to think things through. There is nothing wrong with that. Plan on them being that way, and plan to make it easier for them.

Answer: "I have prepared a one-page summary of the key points. You may want to take this back to the office (only if you want to) and kick it around a bit with the boss. That's fine. I'll be in my office, so if you want to sneak in an E-mail or catch me in between your meetings, I'll be sure to call you back."

Legitimize his secretiveness and suggest that you can be confided in.

Type 3. The "You're the Expert, Dummy" Client

Client: "So, what do you think we should do? I can't spend all my time educating you. It's been a long time already. You're the expert. What's the answer?"

Response: This client is giving in to his or her inclination to dominate you. It's pointless to speculate why. It could be a fear, it could be resentment, or it could just be that he's having a bad day. Don't call his bluff, or you'll embarrass him as much as yourself. Instead, give back value in the form of a number of hypotheses.

Answer: "Well, I know what the answer has been for a number of other clients, but each was different. You've got real choices available to you here. I would like to do a little more exploring on this because it could go a number of different ways. I think it depends on a few things; may we talk just a little more?"

Type 4. The "Let Me Handle That" Client

Client: "This is good stuff, but you don't know the politics. You'd get chewed up. They don't understand you yet. It's a little risky.

Give me this stuff, I'll take care of it. I'll run interference on the politics. Let me handle that."

Response: This is the language of a client who doesn't trust you. Your first route is to apply the trust skills and trust process, and see if you can earn the right to represent them in political as well as technical areas. However, this may also be the language of a client who doesn't trust *anyone*. So your second route may be to try naming and claiming, in a private conversation, about how secure the person feels in the job; security is a deep-seated reason for someone holding on to contacts rather than delegating them.

> *Answer:* "That's really interesting; I can see much of what you're saying, but I'm not sure about all of it. Can you take a few minutes to tell me more about it?"

Type 5. The "Let's Go Through This Again" Client

Client: "The fifth draft is coming along well, but the nuances are what kill you. You know, the devil is in the details. These rehearsal drafts are really key, especially for the staff committees."

Response (frame via alternatives): Clients like this are most comfortable in the detail realm. They have probably learned to add some reasonable value in that realm, so don't discard it completely. On the other hand, this detail orientation probably masks a desire to control things, which can get in the way of big-picture approaches. Your solution is to make the big picture "feel" controllable.

> *Answer:* "Should we spend 40 percent on big picture and 60 percent on detail, or the reverse?" or "Let's use this well-known five-step model to walk through the big picture in detail."

Type 6. The "You Don't Understand" Client

Client: "You don't understand our business. You're from *East* Slobovia, not *West* Slobovia, so of course you wouldn't appreciate things. You haven't been around here for long, so you wouldn't get that."

Response: This client, like any human being, wants to feel special. The truth is, the *more* clients perceive similarities with other businesses, the *more* confident they will become that their own experience serves them well in the world. But you can't argue. You'll have plenty of time to demonstrate the similarities during the relationship, but you have to start where this person is starting.

Don't try to win this battle head-on. Acknowledge that you're from East Slobovia; you're sure it's different out here. You're not sure just how, but you hope the person will help you on that road, and in due time you will assess together how critically deficient your lack of knowledge is.

> *Answer:* "I'm sure that's exactly right. Would you be willing to help me understand what's different here? I'm really keen to learn, so that I can at least try to be useful. Could you share with me a few of the things I need to know?"

Type 7. The "My Enemy's Enemy Is My Friend" Client

Client: "So, what does this mean for Alison? And you know it's not going to play in Richmond. Don't mention this to the folks in legal, what they don't know can't hurt them. And what did Bill think about this recommendation?"

Response: These clients love politics. Perhaps this is their way of seeking out an internal area of power or leverage in which there is less competition than in the content area. Regardless, you can speak their language and serve both them and you well.

Don't debate the value of what they say, and don't criticize it. Instead, make politics a content issue. Talk about it freely, albeit with the door closed, with an agenda, objectives, pros and cons, all the trappings of investment or marketing discussions. If it is in fact inappropriate to discuss such and such an issue, then they will be forced to shut down the conversation, but without you having forced them to, and without overtly shaming them.

> *Answer:* "OK, that sounds important; let's go through it. What stake does Alison have in this? Please help me understand precisely what won't play in Richmond. Could you please give me some guidelines on what can and can't go to legal? Bill was fine with this. Why do you ask?"

Type 8. The "Just Like, You Know, Come On" Client

Client: "I want you to, uh, you know, make it happen. A clear statement of it. It's a simple proposition. We just need help to make it work, manage it, make it happen, you know. Write that up, what I just said."

Response: Some people's strengths just aren't in the verbal arena. Such clients often have counterbalancing strengths in clarity of insight, or have communication skills that are far less verbal.

Join and help them. Don't force them to work in *your* comfort zone. Give them alternatives. Write *something* up. People who can't articulate their needs have a logjam of needs to express. You need to give them voice. Write up options they can react to by ranking or rating. Don't expect open-ended questions to work. If they can't explain in open-ended terms what they want, why should more open questions help? Don't get frustrated. You have a great opportunity to add value by reducing their lifelong frustration, and make yourself invaluable in the process.

> *Answer:* "I took a stab at writing up something on what we talked about the other day. This is a full outline, though it's only a draft; I wanted to bounce it off you before we start going final on it. Which part do you like best? Least?"

Type 9. The "Oh, By the Way" Client

> *Client:* "Oh, by the way, I probably should have invited you to that meeting we just had. Did you read the piece? I probably should have sent it to you. You probably should have been involved in that project, but hey, do the best you can."

Response: Are you consistently missing out on key initiatives, meetings, memos, or data? One of two things is going on. Either the client has some kind of personal issue with you, or you are unaware that the client sees you as carrying around a very large label on your forehead, proclaiming you to be an expert in XYZ area but having not a clue outside it. Either way, you are likely to feel insulted. Don't be.

Ask for a private meeting. Assume that you are being labeled, not that the client doesn't like you. Use all the best naming and claiming techniques. Ask the client to help you stand in his shoes. Edit your language to make sure that not a single phrase enters it that sounds like "we really think" or "I'd like to" or "we're good at" or "we want."

This client doesn't care what you think, or like, or want. And he won't, and shouldn't, until he has some reason to believe that you have a clue about non-XYZ issues. This client needs to be engaged (see Chapter 10). If the issue really is that the client doesn't like you, he's likely to tell you, rather than leaving you twisting in the wind. Even a client who doesn't like you isn't likely to continue lying to you if you're sincere.

> *Answer:* "Thanks for meeting me. I asked for this brief time to-gether because I'm missing some data, without which I can't be of much help. There have been five occasions of my missing a meet-ing, document, or study, and I'm not clear why that is. What would I have to do to get in the loop? I really want to help make a difference around here, and I would like to work together with you and support your efforts. I am prepared to do whatever it takes. I apologize if this is a difficult conversation (it is for me as well), but my guess is we'll all be better off if we're candid. Does that make sense to you? If so, can you help me understand what I can do to be sure I'm being effective?"

17

The Lieutenant Columbo Approach

SOMETIMES A METAPHOR MORE CONCISELY captures and conveys meaning better than can be done by a collection of words. Such may be the case with the television character Lieutenant Columbo, who embodies a number of characteristics that can be useful for successful advisors.

For the uninitiated, Lt. Columbo is a television character, played by Peter Falk successfully for three decades. Columbo is a detective in the Los Angeles Police Homicide Bureau. By all rights, this ought to make him an imposing character. Yet he is anything but.

In the *Columbo* episodes, we are privy from the start to the insider's view of the crime. We know who the criminal is. Thus, unlike Perry Mason, we are not caught up in the game of playing detective. The game in which we are caught up is that of watching a master detective play the game of uncovering the truth.

And how he plays it! From the start, Columbo has his (correct) suspicions. And inevitably, the criminal begins to let his (or her) guard down. The criminals begin convinced that they are invincible; as time goes on, it appears that luck conspires against them. Of course, it isn't luck at all. It is Columbo's death grasp.

The key to Columbo lies in his style and, perhaps, even his character. It does not lie in his method. This is the first parallel to successful consulting. He disdains official police methodology, preferring to go for customized, on-off, situational gut-feel and instinct, in the belief that his behavior will lead the criminal to let down his guard.

Columbo's style is informal, even sloppy, to a fault. He drives an old Peugeot, wears a rumpled trench coat, and continually smokes what look like very cheap cigars. His gestures are familiar ones of befuddlement, distraction, puzzlement, and inability to process information. He appears overwhelmed and underqualified. As such, he usually appears dazzled by the fame, style, and/or sheer brilliance of the criminal he is stalking.

Of course, he is none of these things. His style is very studiously chosen. He frequently asks to use the restroom, a very humanizing touch calculated to put the criminal at ease. We often hear of his wife, but never hear her name. As far as we know, her first name is "Mrs."

At the surface level, Columbo appears incompetent. Just to be clear, we do not for a moment suggest that one should adopt an appearance and demeanor of incompetence. But consider what is going on just one level below the surface.

Columbo uses his style to eradicate a preconception, thereby setting the other party at ease. This is his genius, and this is what an advisor must emulate. Consider the typical client, who is sometimes intimidated by the technical expertise of the advisor, which by definition far exceeds his own. A common client feeling (however unconscious) is one of "you expert, me dummy." This sends out psychological echoes many levels deep. Those echoes may include resentment, awe, jealousy, identification, competition, desire to be liked, and so on.

On top of that, the client approaches typically with a problem, an issue that is troubling and that needs solving. So there are things at stake, either costs or potential benefits, things to be lost or things yet to be gained. This produces yet another level of psychological echoes, a sense of criticality, of impending something.

Finally, there are the trappings of the meeting. The framed degree behind the advisor's desk, the white lab coat, the latest electronic business toy, the thumb-worn copy of the Official Airline Guide. These are all visible symbols that reinforce the sense of one's fate being in the hands of another.

Columbo knows all this, and punctures it neatly. He praises the "client's" intelligence. He wears the anti-uniform. He makes small talk. He dismisses the seriousness of his capabilities. And one by one, the "client's" inhibitions and concerns begin to vanish.

In this environment, Columbo is ready to go to work. The

"client" is now willing to talk openly and honestly. He begins to describe things as he perceives them and not as he wants others to perceive them. Information is offered rather than withheld. Personalities emerge for what they are. And progress toward resolution can be made.

On one level, Columbo's lesson is obvious. Set the client at ease and don't overwhelm him with technical expertise. But part of Columbo's fascination for us is that it is not easy, at all, to emulate him. What are the obstacles to Columbo-based consulting?

The biggest barrier is our own love, as advisors, for all the things that put the client on guard. The degrees, the uniforms, and the other trappings of our professions signify success: We worked hard, extremely hard, to get where we got and, by golly, what's wrong with a little discrete demonstration of our status?

If we can overcome that need for ego gratification, another big barrier appears. That is, of course, the belief that our success is exclusively about technical mastery. So we behave in anti-Columbo ways by continually nodding sagely, and interpolating pieces of knowledgeable wisdom (the professional equivalent of name-dropping.) We listen with our noses high, until we deign to descend with the almighty Answer (or so it can seem to our clients). Don't forget, many of our clients believe in this game as well; at least until they are faced with something better.

The biggest barrier to capitalizing on Columbo's wisdom, then, is once again found through Pogo's dictum: We have found the enemy, and it is us. It is our own inability to act upon the so-called marketing principle, that we should focus on our clients and their problems exclusively, and not letting our own personalities, needs and, images get in the way.

Columbo's genius lies in neutralizing expectations about himself. He is not a trickster; he is the anti-trickster. He is not an illusionist; he is the one who strips away illusions. He becomes the professional equivalent of beige, of background music. He subordinates his ego to the service of the client.

And, of course, he always wins.

18

The Role of Trust in Getting Hired

DALTON WAS A (disguised) management-consulting firm with an excellent process for new client selling. It pioneered the application of industrial sales techniques to professional services. It disproved conclusively the idea rampant in the professions that the person who sells the work is the only person the client wants to do the work.

Dalton had a four-step sales and service process, with entirely different people and organizational units at each step in the process. It worked staggeringly well for a number of years, but the successful sales model turned out to hold the seeds of its own destruction.

Part of Dalton's genius was to create specialists in lead generation, specialists in closing, specialists in diagnostics, and specialists in delivery. All were distinct parts of the organization, with distinct measurement and reward systems. And all were very professional and competent in a new client situation.

The delivery organization viewed its job, not surprisingly, as delivering results that were at least as good as, and preferably better than, the client's expectations in terms of budget, deliverables, timing, and benefits from both revenue enhancement and cost savings. They did *not* perceive selling to be part of their job, since that was the task of the other three divisions of the organization.

The lead generation group, not surprisingly, viewed their task as one of identifying and qualifying new clients. They didn't see it as their job to call on existing clients; and in fact the other three parts of the organization would probably have resented it if they had. Ditto for the "closers" and the diagnosticians. Their job was to process the leads from the step before them.

The delivery team saw its job as executing a defined specification and budget. They thought of themselves as professionals, and took pride in the work they did. But their definition of professionalism rarely included the idea that they should be on the lookout for other opportunities for improvement the client might have.

The clients didn't usually think about expansion opportunities or follow-on work. When they did, they tended to focus on the delivery organization, with whom they were most acquainted and with whom they worked daily. But that group was not skilled at selling, and in fact viewed selling as a detriment to and distraction from meeting their primary goal: delivery on time and on budget.

The result was a perpetually low client retention machine. Profitability and margins were rather low, but as long as a steady flow of new clients kept growth high, no one much minded. However, when demand for Dalton's primary service line declined somewhat, and when Dalton began to run out of prime category clients, the engine began to run out of steam, and Dalton's fortunes rapidly declined.

While the case of Dalton Consulting might show that selling and service don't have to coexist in the same person, it reveals that there needs to be a mechanism to relate them. This case study is about much more than the failure of an existing-client sales program. It is about how the two capabilities are integrally related.

The point is *not* that you can't have specialized organizations around the functions of sales and service. We think Dalton made some important innovations in this regard. What the case *does* say is that there must be *some* way to combine the professional perspective of always seeking different opportunities with that of seeking excellence in delivering that which has already been noticed. Having the two roles in one person or in one organizational unit are fairly obvious ways to achieve that combination.

Integrating Sales and Service

While most professionals would not go so far as Dalton, they would nevertheless acknowledge a significant difference between selling one's services and providing the service. First we get the client to agree to the work (that's selling). Then we do the work (that's serving). What could be more clear?

But the more you try to define the difference, the harder it gets to make the distinction. How does one sell? By demonstrating (not asserting) to a client that we have something to offer and that we are someone in whom they can place their trust. These are essentially serving actions.

How does one serve? Serving means helping the client and meeting his or her needs in such a way that the client is delighted, wants to hire us again, and tells all their friends and business acquaintances about us. What is that if not selling?

The truth is, sales and service, when thought of properly, converge. The two are flip sides of the same coin. And the name of that coin is acting like a trusted advisor and a caring professional.

Service as Selling

Most advisors are a little uncomfortable with overt selling. They would like to believe that the quality of their work speaks for itself, that the need for their services is self-evident to the client and that it is therefore unnecessary to belabor the obvious in selling. Alas, this is not always true.

However, if we think of the task not as selling ("How do I push what we've got"), but as getting hired ("How do I convince this person to put his or her trust in me?"), then the required activities become a great deal clearer.

Imagine the following scenario: You are invited, along with three competitors, to participate in a "beauty contest," a competition among firms to gain a significant contract or piece of business. The client is not a service novice and is quite willing to give you (and your competitors) considerable pre-presentation access to several of their key people. End-runs, however, are frowned upon.

The client makes it quite clear that a decision will be made from among several firms and that the decision will be based largely on what they hear at a final presentation. Up to three hours are allotted to each firm. How should you spend your three hours? You could, of course, do the standard presentation. Or you could dress it up with a number of techniques to enhance presentational effectiveness, many of which are very sound.

There is another option, however. Get to work immediately! Use the allotted three hours as the first three hours of the scheduled project. The logic of this approach is simple. In professional services, where the "good" being bought is not only expensive but also intangible and often vague, the seller who succeeds is the seller who can show the buyer just what it feels like to be in a relationship together.

This is because most buyers of professional services, even relatively experienced ones, are quite aware of a number of risks. There is financial risk, emotional risk, the risk of lost time, the risk of embarrassment in case of a wrong decision, career risk, and so on. An advisor who can reduce all those risks by demonstrating (with visceral impact) how it will feel to work together is at a significant advantage. This is also why the individual (or firm) with the relationship has such an advantage in professional services: "The devil you know is better than the one you don't."

Hence the best selling technique is to not sell, but to commence the service process. Many professionals, in their business development activities, will *talk about* serving, rather than actually serving. ("It's going to be wonderful once you start paying, we promise you. But we won't show you anything until money changes hands.")

One of the worst forms of self-delusion is to assume that one is selling specialized knowledge and that there is a limited amount of it to go around. This preconception leads professionals to resist invitations to take a point of view, to refuse to go out on a limb. Through a combination of fear and of belief that you shouldn't "give away" the goods until the client has paid, the professional loses both new work and a relationship.

The professions, in a sense, sell confidence, security, and ease. No client wants to buy air unless they can breathe it first. No client wants to buy a painting without seeing it. If given any choice at all, clients prefer to buy based on a sample.

Selling as Service

Most of us would agree that, if we see something bad about to happen to our clients, we have a professional obligation to point out the situation to them. And it is not much of a stretch to say that we should therefore do the same if we see a significant opportunity for improvement.

Do we also agree that all of our clients, at any point in time, are far from perfect, that they are all faced with a great number of opportunities for improvement across a number of dimensions? If that is the case, don't we have some professional obligation to continually keep an eye out for those opportunities to the best of our ability? Then why do we act on it so rarely?

To be professional, we must point out possibilities. Some call that selling. We call it contributing ideas. Good selling requires giving the client a taste of what it feels like to work together. That feels like serving. Good sales is good service is good sales, and so on.

There is very little difference between what we have just described as a professional obligation, and what someone else might call selling. After all, both involve noticing a legitimate opportunity for improvement, and raising the awareness of the client about the significance and benefits of taking the action suggested.

Frequently, it seems that advisors don't just leave business on the table, they actually leave opportunities for clients unnoted. This means that, to some extent, they are behaving unprofessionally. In order to behave in a more professional manner, we must understand what gets in the way of pointing out client opportunities.

The real link is between the ethos of selling and the ethos of serving. To act professionally, an advisor must at all times have the client's best interests at heart.

19

Building Trust
on the Current Assignment

IN *MANAGING THE PROFESSIONAL SERVICE FIRM,* David outlined some of the factors that increase a client's perceived value of service. These were:

1. Understanding
2. Sense of control
3. Sense of progress
4. Access and availability
5. Responsiveness
6. Reliability
7. Appreciation
8. Sense of importance
9. Respect

All of this, done well, promote the client's trust in the advisor. Notice that, for example, it is not enough that we actually do respect the client. We should also act in such a way that the client *experiences* the fact that we respect him or her. How is this done? One way, for example, is to ask (regularly) for the client's opinion.

Some other tactics to build trust on the assignment include:

1. Involving the client in the process through:
   - brainstorming sessions
   - giving the client tasks to perform
   - giving the client options and letting the client choose

- keeping the client informed on what's going to happen, when, and why

2. Making reports and presentations more useful and easier to pass on by:

   - getting the client to instruct us on format and presentation

   - providing a summary so the client can use it internally without modification

   - having all reports read by a non-project person to ensure readability and comprehension prior to delivery

   - providing all charts, tables, and summaries on overheads for internal client use

3. Helping the client use what we deliver by:

   - coaching the client in dealing with others in client organization

   - empowering the client with reasoning steps

   - advising on tactics/politics of how results should be shared inside client organization

   - writing progress summaries in a way that the client can use internally without modification

4. Making meetings more valuable by:

   - establishing specific agenda and goals prior to meeting

   - sending information and reports in advance, saving meeting time for discussion, not presentation

   - finding out attendees in advance and researching them

   - establishing next steps for both sides

   - dictating and transcribing a summary of all meetings and significant phone conversations and sending copy to client the same day or next day

   - calling afterward to confirm that goals were met

5. Being accessible and available by:

   - calling in advance when we know we're going to be unavailable

   - ensuring that our assistants know where we are and when we'll be back

   - ensuring that our assistants know the names of all clients and names of all team members involved in the relationship

- working at getting clients comfortable with our "junior" personnel, so they can be available when we're not

All of these tactics are small gestures, and they cannot all be used in all situations. However, by using these and similar actions frequently, we can demonstrate that we are trying to make life easier for our client, and trying to meet his or her needs in relation to both content and process. If the client sees us trying to anticipate and respond to his or her needs, we will maintain and possibly grow the degree of trust we have.

Building Trust During the Engagement Process

Serving a client does not just mean going away, doing the work, and coming back with a wonderful product that you expect them to praise. Instead, we must keep clients up to date, continue to ask them questions that show we're working on it for real, and build their input quite visibly into our work product. This shows we're still (and always) listening to them.

Building trust does not mean saying it's all easy or hiding the hard stuff from clients. It means letting them know the thorniest, most troublesome parts of the assignment (not to whine, but to ask them if this was their impression, too).

We must make sure we can see how the particular assignment fits into a larger perspective, how it affects what else they're trying to accomplish from a broader standpoint, and letting them know (maybe only once!) that we've drawn that connection. This constitutes framing on one level, adds to credibility on another, and also helps envision an alternate reality by making connections.

Stop to make sure you're still in touch with the client, perhaps just to check in with them personally. Ask about what else they're up to or worried about. This creates intimacy, by showing we care enough to stop the urgent work at hand and focus on the individual as a person.

We should also ask them who else in their organization might be a "tough sell" on what they're trying to accomplish, and try to build some "barrier busters" into either our work product or how the work product is introduced to the organization. By getting involved and thinking ahead about the internal implementation of our recommendations, we are taking a "we-not-me" approach, and helping to envision the alternate reality.

We should learn the names of the clients' support and administrative staff. We should learn them well, early, and thoroughly. It impresses people, and it may result in a few favors along the way. It also exhibits caring behavior. On a deeper level, it will make us more familiar and more comfortable with the client organization.

We should read over our past notes from time to time, looking for issues that were raised but have yet to be addressed. Then we can go back and talk about them. Even if nothing ends up getting done, it will show we listen and that we cared enough to return to the issue at hand.

We should occasionally bring in an item of interest from outside the topic of the current assignment. We shouldn't be the sole judge of what is useful, but should involve the client in that decision. If it's even possibly interesting, we should bring it up. We'll learn something either way. This models "we-not-me" and shows that we're thinking of them and are occasionally willing to take a risk for them in terms of relevance.

When in doubt, we should share information. We should err on the side of more communication, not less; more advance notice, not less; more people in the loop, not fewer. Certainly there are times for discretion, but not all times require it. Sharing information shows respect for including the client in the decision regarding relevance, and it enhances credibility by showing that we have nothing to hide.

We should find ways to make many small commitments, then meet them. Examples: "I'll have that to you by 5 P.M.," "I'll call you at noon," "Let me make sure Jimmy gets that too," "I saw an article on that; I'll be sure to get it to you." As we have argued, reliability, and thus trust, is built not on elapsed time but on accumulated experiences.

We must be prepared to deal with the client's ever-changing mind. We can be sure that circumstances will change from the point at which our assignment begins to the point it is completed. As our client's situation evolves and changes, we should expect our client's goals and mind to change as well.

If we do not anticipate that our clients will change their minds about some elements of the transaction, we are likely to have a conflict with them when it begins to happen. Our representation of a client is a continuum, and what may have started as the appropriate goal for the client at the beginning of the assignment may be totally inappropriate as it nears the end.

Following our initial courtship with a client, we begin to enter a very short honeymoon period, where the client feels relieved that someone competent is now at work solving his or her problem. There is a natural evolution to the relationship where those feelings of comfort will quickly transform into feelings of wondering whether their advisor is devoting the time necessary and whether the approach is really going to work.

Trust is built upon respect, and since respect comes from seeing some performance, it becomes imperative that we find the means to deliver a small, fast result to evidence our efforts. We must make something happen, and make it happen quickly.

There are times, however, when the nature of the assignment does not lend itself to quick results. In those instances, even compiling a status report can ensure our credibility. From sending the client a brief update to calling at home over the weekend, we need to find different means of demonstrating that we are out there making our best efforts on the client's behalf. Other thoughts:

1. We must always keep clients in the loop regarding our progress. We should not wait to bowl them over with blinding insights at the end. Chances are, the insights won't be that blinding. Also, if the conclusions are likely to surprise the client, we shouldn't try to use drama to dazzle. There's nothing worse than an angry client who feels "surprised" by findings (even if the findings are good), particularly if they're delivered in a semipublic forum or meeting. When we fail to meet agreements we made with a client (not meeting a deadline, going over the budget, falling short of the result we promised), we compromise any trust that we are attempting to develop. Worse yet, if we suggest to our client that perhaps the deadline, the budget, or the result promised were a bit unrealistic, we compromise completely our credibility.

With deadlines and fee quotes, we must be careful of what we promise. Trusted advisors recognize that they can get into trouble by wanting to make a good impression and promising more than they can deliver. Clients often forget the promises we keep but remember the promises we didn't fulfill.

2. We must always tell the truth and not what the client wants to hear. One of the greatest dangers to the client relationship is telling the client what he or she wants to hear, rather than what is in his or her best interests. Clients can get especially frustrated and disappointed when advisors refuse to accept responsibility, even for unintentional acts. Hearing, "It was not my fault," or "But that was not my intention" strikes clients as a lame defense. They consider it an abdication of responsibility, a diversion of blame, and an infraction in the trust relationship.

3. We should love our work. Let the client see our enthusiasm. Cool is OK. Passion is even more OK.

4. We should always try to make sure that our answer is not a purely technical one. And always ask how our work affects the client individually and personally. What are the financial implications? What are the job or role or career implications? We need to be eternally alert for what comes next for the client. What should our client be doing as a result of our work? Create the follow-on plan for them (at no charge) even if we're not involved in the follow-on. They then might well call us for our counsel. In fact, the chances are good that they will.

5. Don't ask for follow-on work too quickly. Eager is good. Aggressive is not.

Here are the top five things that can destroy trust on an engagement:

1. *Compromising the confidences of an individual.* Giving away secrets to show how "in the know" you are is not a wise move. We all want to be viewed as credible. Being in the loop is one manifestation of that. But it comes at a price. People will forgive someone for not being in the know. They won't forgive someone for misusing information. Especially an outsider.

2. *Not picking up the sense that a client may have questions, uncertainties, or unhappiness about a certain aspect of your work.* Once, many

years ago, Charlie and Rob had a small piece of work with a very tight deadline for a major investment-banking firm, and it happened at a time when things were very busy (for Rob, Charlie and the client).

The key client (who, we told ourselves repeatedly afterward, was impatient and imperious) had a concern about the final product. It was not about the content, but about the format. Charlie and Rob pointed out that the content was right, and they tried to make light of the fact that only the format was the issue. It didn't matter to the client, who subsequently decided that if the format wasn't acceptable, neither was the content. Needless to say, the relationship didn't develop any further.

3. *Going around (or behind) the client to get something done, even if it was something important.* It's just not worth it. People always find out. Assume that nothing stays secret for very long.

4. *Engaging in "I am sometimes wrong, but I am never in doubt" behavior.* People just hate that sort of thing. Even if someone is well wired into the senior client, that behavior alienates the rest of the client organization faster than just about anything else. Rob remembers a particular young tax lawyer whose vehemence was part of his stock-in-trade. It was fascinating to watch, over time, just how many promising relationships initiated by this individual ended up in failure.

5. *Blowing a deadline that's important to the client.* Even if it's an artificial deadline, even if it's arbitrary, it's their deadline unless they explicitly say otherwise. If it's an unreasonable one, it's better to ask for an extension, or even argue about it. If the product is still going to be late, better to let it be known in advance than to deliver it late without warning. If a client is angry but forewarned, there's only one thing to be worried about. If a client is angry and not forewarned, there's *much* to be worried about!

20

Re-earning Trust Away from the Current Assignment

TRUST AND RELATIONSHIPS are built not only by activities connected to the current assignment. There are many opportunities to build your relationship with your client outside the demands of the current work.

In order to help professional firms design and implement programs for relationship management, David has interviewed clients of firms representing a wide variety of professions and countries, to obtain their view of their relationships with their outside providers.

Many of these clients' concerns are similar. A few of the more commonly expressed client concerns are:

- They are only interested in selling their services, not solving our problems.

- They don't do anything to make us feel our business is important to them. We are taken completely for granted. They never call up to inquire how our business is doing. We only see them when they want to sell something.

- There are few signs that they're really listening to us. They bring us generic issues faced by all companies. We want to hear about the specific opportunities for, and challenges facing, our company.

- We don't want to be "romanced." We already have many opportunities to go to fancy dinners or attend sporting events. They should focus on being useful to us, not on becoming our friends.

A number of key conclusions can be drawn from this list. It is clear that clients want their providers to *continually earn* their future business. Relationships cannot be taken for granted. It is equally clear that they don't want a "sales pitch." Instead, the emphasis must be placed on investing the advisor's own (non-reimbursed) time to build the relationship. This is not always done. Rather than a relationship plan, many advisors draw up sales plans. The difference is readily apparent to clients.

What Clients Want

What *do* clients want advisors to do to grow their relationship? Here are a few of the most commonly expressed client suggestions:

1. Make an impact on our business, don't just be visible.
2. Do more things "on spec" (i.e., invest your time on preliminary work in new areas).
3. Spend more time helping us think, and helping us develop strategies.
4. Lead our thinking. Tell us what our business is going to look like five or ten years from now.
5. *Jump* on any new pieces of information we have, so you can stay up-to-date on what's going on in our business. Use our data to give us an extra level of analysis. Ask for it, don't wait for us to give it to you.
6. Schedule some offsite meetings together. Join us for brainstorming sessions about our business.
7. Make an extra effort to understand how our business works: sit in on our meetings.
8. Help us see how we compare to others, both within and outside our industry.
9. Tell me why our competitors are doing what they're doing.
10. Discuss with us other things we should be doing; we welcome any and all ideas!

What many of these suggestions have in common is that they are about expending serious effort on getting to know the client's business and industry in great depth, and being proactive in offering suggestions for improvement. Some of this can take place in the professional firm's "back room" (conducting studies, benchmarking, etc.). However, much will require greater (nonpaid) contact with the client. It is notable that while clients want more contact, they want it to be in settings that allow mutual discussions and explorations of the issues.

It is also clear that clients want a business partner, not a false friend. The good news is that clients clearly do want us to bring them new ideas, and that they *want* a relationship.

Stay in Touch

Clients' comments clearly indicate that they want us to stay in touch. This is contrary to the instincts of many advisors (like our friend Rebecca in Chapter 15), who feel as though they are imposing on the client if they call when there is not a "live" project.

The truth is there's nothing more destructive to trust than to call only when we want something. Great trusted advisors stay in regular contact with their clients, even if they are not currently working on a project for that client.

To maintain trust when the project is over, we must recognize that it's never over, as long as we check in. The impact of our work continues long after we are gone, and in ways we often can't imagine. It is never too late to reestablish a relationship, even if significant time has elapsed. It may be harder as time goes by, but it is never too late!

Creating Institutional Relationships

Among large firms with large clients, there is often a desire to try to build institutional relationships. As we have noted, trust is personal, not institutional, but that does not mean that this goal is impossible. If a professional firm wishes to develop an institutional relationship with a major client, it requires more than a single member of the firm (the relationship manager) focusing his or her attention on a few key decision makers.

A proper relationship with a major "account" (a word that we dislike, for what we hope are obvious reasons) requires the full participation of a large number of people who service or deal with the client. Everyone who participates in serving the client can, and does, affect the relationship. Multiple contacts must be established, and a *consistency* of service and attentiveness must be attained. It's no good if each provider behaves in different ways, since a firm-

wide reputation is built only if each person can be trusted and relied upon to operate to the same standards.

Clearly, clients *want* their outside providers to recognize their
specific needs and opportunities, and to customize any suggestions
for additional work. This also requires teamwork among all of the
outside firm's people, since the key relationship manager is often
poorly positioned to identify the client's emerging issues.

It is often the case that the client CEO and other headquarters
personnel are among the last ones to know about emerging issues.
Frequently, it is the client's junior executives and "field" people
who are most aware of developing issues, and most willing to talk
openly about them. Accordingly, junior professionals on the provider's team, who have the greatest contact with these people during the current engagement, are often best positioned to surface
new needs.

Many firms have developed such systems of relationship managers who are responsible for the firm's total relationship with each
key client. These individuals have the responsibility of managing
(and growing) their firm's relationship with major clients, coordi-
nating professionals across the various disciplines of the firm, and
often across geographic boundaries.

To make such a system work, the relationship manager must act
as the client's representative to the firm (perhaps even the client's
advocate), ensuring that all of the firm's resources are brought to
bear on the client's problems. The logic of this should be clear: If we
ensure that the client's needs are met, the firm will benefit.

Relationship managers are most effective when they focus on
the (long-term) issue of strengthening the *relationship*. Where relationship managers see themselves primarily as salespeople, primarily focused on generating more fees from the client, they are
less well accepted by the client and become less effective.

Many relationship managers see their role as carrying the primary burden of building the trust relationship between themselves
as individuals and various client executives. This is usually a mistake. The most important part of a relationship officer's job is to
manage the relationship, not to try to build it alone. He or she must
be active in creating opportunities for other members of the professional firm's team to meet with additional client executives and
begin new trust relationships.

This can be done by offering to put on free internal seminars for the client organization, where new members of the professional firm have the chance to demonstrate their expertise and to meet other client personnel in a low-stress (non-selling) environment. An alternate approach is to offer the services of a colleague to attend a client's internal meeting (for free) as a way of both investing in the relationship (and being seen to do so) and opening the door for new relationships to form by new people meeting each other.

Part of the job of the relationship manager is to create and energize the team serving their mutual client. This means devoting significant time to being a terrific coach.

The relationship manager's task is to make the team members *want* to participate actively in serving and nurturing the relationship (not the "account"). This can be done by providing what they often do not find in their regular work, such as challenge and meaning. In principle, work for key clients should be exciting and challenging, even more than serving other kinds of clients.

However, meaning and challenge should not be taken for granted. Amid the hurly-burly of busy professional lives, it is easy to lose sight of the significance of what one is working on. Effective relationship managers work at helping their team members find the excitement, the challenge and the drama in this client's problems.

Effective relationship managers also work hard to make the people on their team look good. They create opportunities for other team members to participate in high-visibility activities that help their careers. They are willing to suppress their own ego needs and to work hard to give the team members valuable client exposure so they can begin to build their own trust relationships. Great relationship managers work hard to create new contacts for the team members, and they get them involved in stretching, learning activities that are out of the norm of the team members' daily lives.

Since the best way to get someone to cooperate with you is to do them a favor first, great relationship managers work hard to serve their team *before* they need to call on them. They work on the principle that if they serve their team well, the team will serve the client.

Outstanding relationship managers think about ways to make it easier for their team to serve the client. They give them tools, research, and industry and client information, all in an easily digested form. They arrange for someone to read, summarize, and circulate *every* trade magazine, industry association publication, and financial analyst report in their client's industry, so that all team members are up-to-date about what's going on in the client's world.

The most important fact to note about relationship management off the current assignment is that it is an investment activity for everyone involved. Significant (non-reimbursed) budgets must be set aside, and the relationship management program launched with a longer-term perspective than the traditional professional firm "fee credits" or "bookings" systems usually allow.

The best news is that relationship management is in everyone's interests. Clients want it, and it benefits the firm by growing relationships and generating new fees. Done properly, it can also provide career-enhancing opportunities for every professional involved. Studies in many industries have proven that there is a clear link between profitability and success in nurturing relationships. It's hard work, but it's a clear path to economic success.

21

The Case of Cross-Selling

CROSS-SELLING BY DEFINITION REFERS to selling within an organization that is, at some level, already a client. Of necessity, it involves a mixture of new people as individual clients, and/or new service offerings (and hence often new people) from the professional firm side. Consequently, *new relationships* are at the very heart of cross-selling.

Since cross-selling starts with an existing advisor serving an existing client, it would seem, at first blush, to be perfectly suited to promote relationships. In reality (as we shall see), we have two strangers trying to get to know each other, each carrying a heavy burden of real and presumed reputations and expectations. Cross-selling is as much about strangers as it is about relationships. Yet the critical sales events are between those who know each other the best! No wonder cross-selling feels hard, to both sides. It is not what it appears to be.

Trust is mainly personal, not institutional, and is not very transferable. An advisor can help a colleague in getting the advisor's client to trust the colleague, but it's not easy. The deeper the trust between advisor and client, the more likely that the client will take the advisor's word that the colleague is trustworthy. But it will rarely be enough.

Cross-selling is like meeting your prospective in-laws for the first time: They'll probably like you, but you'd better not take it for granted. There is more than just one relationship at stake!

In some people's view of cross-selling, there is the expectation that an institutional relationship can transmit trust. It cannot. Trust is personal. When the presumption of institutional transferability confronts the reality of strangers meeting, all are left with an uncomfortable feeling.

Types of Cross-Selling

There is a very old model originally used to map old/new customers against old/new products. That model is easily adaptable to reflect typical cross-selling situations, as shown in Figure 21-1.

Type 1 cross-selling (as shown in the diagram) refers to the attempt to introduce a new service offering to a current client individual; the new player is the professional firm's new content expert. (Let's call this type Expand.)

Type 2 cross-selling is when an existing service is being offered to a new person in the client organization (perhaps a different division of an existing client); the new player is the new client individual. (We'll call this Broaden.)

Type 3 cross-selling involves two new players, one from each side. The professional firm is trying to sell a new service to a new person in the client organization. (This will be Diversify.)

Before we start analyzing these, let's repeat here the trust equation calculations from Chapter 8, which we use as a baseline to compare the levels of trust in each situation.

Fig. 21.1. The Three Cross-Selling Types

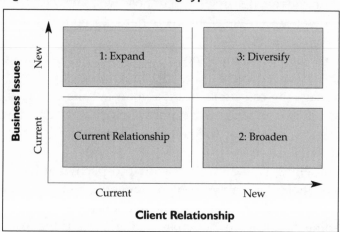

Current Trust Score

$$T = (C + R + I) / S$$

$$T = (5 + 3 + 2) / 8 = 1.25 \text{ new client}$$

$$T = (7 + 8 + 5) / 4 = 5 \text{ current client}$$

To make it easier, let's take it one step at a time, looking first at the Type 1 cross-sell situation.

Type 1 (Expand)

Suppose that Amy (a current advisor) wants to pitch a new service offering (which will involve her colleague, Barbara) to her existing client, Curt:

Let's listen in on some typical thoughts of these key cross-sale players.

AMY: I just *know* I can help Curt with the new service, if I can only get him to hook up with Barbara, our expert in that area.

CURT: I think of Amy's firm as people who do what they're doing for me. I don't associate them with this new area. And I don't know Barbara.

Amy, the existing-service relationship manager, has a conversation with her current client, Curt, in a scenario called "Passing the Business Card."

"Curt, you and I both know you've got a new issue around here. It's an important one, and a lot is at stake. And I know you've talked to Alter Associates about working on it.

"Now the truth is, we also have a lot of expertise in this area, as you know. And I realize there are probably a lot of little reasons why you haven't asked us in to talk about the new issue, but there's too much at stake here for me to be coy or silent.

"I have a colleague named Barbara who is just great at what you need. I really think you should talk to her. I've talked to her about your situation here, and she's got some good ideas. Here's her card. Would you like me to have her call you, or would you prefer to call her at your convenience? Either way is fine by me; let me know."

If you were in Curt's seat, listening to Amy talk, how would you be feeling? You would probably feel that you're being put in a difficult spot; you're are being asked for something without much in return. You probably feel some liberties are being taken.

To sell successfully, trust must grow during the sale. Yet here, trust is being drawn down. It feels to Curt like Amy is asking for a favor (and she is), while offering little in return.

Figure 21-2 rates the trust equation components for this scenario. A numeric score is given, on a 1–10 scale, with qualitative comments. Compare this with the baseline trust level of 5 that prevailed in the preexisting relationship. Quite a drop! In fact, the trust score here is even lower than the hypothetical new client situation in our baseline, a score of 1.25! (As before, if your estimates are different, plug in your own numbers.)

Is it any wonder that Curt is squirming in his seat? Here is someone with whom he is accustomed to dealing at a high trust level, and that person is now making him feel like he does when buying a used car. How unfair! Curt does not even have a graceful

Fig. 21.2. Trust Analysis of Amy, "Passing the Business Card" Scenario

Trust Component	Comment
Credibility: 4	Amy's own credibility on the new content is low; Barbara's only credibility is from Amy, whose motives can seem to be mixed
Reliability: 2	No track record regarding the new service area or Barbara, no plan for getting one
Intimacy: 3	Amy has broadened the agenda to assume shared perspectives on competitors, evaluation of Barbara, and the new area, but all on her own, without involving Curt
Self-orientation: 8	Amy's talk is all about herself, her firm; no indication of focus on client's perspective, issues
Total Trust Score: 1.13	$(C + R + I) / S = $ Trust $(4 + 2 + 3) / 8 = 1.13$

way out. He will probably bury the request, leaving Amy to wonder what happened.

But the situation is even more complicated than that, because the relationship between Amy and Curt is not the only relationship that is relevant here. Amy must deal with Barbara, to persuade her to get involved. We call this the "professional-firm internal sale."

Consider the barriers. First, in many professional firms, Barbara gets less "credit" (formally or informally) for responding to someone else's client than she would for getting someone else to respond to hers. Right away, Barbara's attention must be obtained.

Second, Barbara's time is precious. What assurance does she have that Amy has put in the requisite time qualifying this client? Is she walking into a time-sink?

Third, what about the ever-present risk of embarrassment? Suppose Amy has misidentified the problem, promised too much in terms of results, underestimated in terms of pricing. There is no end to the number of ways in which Amy may have "poisoned" the job before it even starts.

Finally, all this takes place in an environment where Amy and Barbara are colleagues. They may be more or less close personally, but they each know they are supposed to work as a team. This constrains their language; neither can acknowledge self-interest openly.

Amy must create trust around three issues: (1) that the business issue is real and substantial; (2) that she has Barbara's interests at heart as well as her own; and (3) that Barbara is not being set up in any way.

The single best way for Amy to do this is simply to invest a little time in educating Barbara about the client before approaching him (an amount of time slightly above the norm, just enough to be seen as a small sacrifice). This provides Barbara the information to make an informed judgment about whether the business issue is real and whether she can contribute to it. This enhances Amy's *credibility.*

It also shows that Amy is willing to operate from something other than short-term self-interest. She is willing to give up her own time, and to place at risk some of the intimate knowledge of her own client relationship. Thus the time investment also pays off in deeper intimacy between the two of them.

This basic (supposedly simplest) form of cross-selling *can* be made to happen, but only through extensive attention to trust building. Without that, it is a daunting if not impossible task!

Type 2 (Broaden)

This time, Amy, the original advisor, wants to persuade Don, a new client executive, to buy the same service Amy has been providing to Curt, her existing client. What are they thinking?

AMY: I know we can do an excellent job for Don, if Curt will introduce us.

CURT: I'm not sure I want to get involved between Amy and Don.

Here is Amy in "I Just Need an Intro."

"Curt, you and I both know that Don's group could use exactly what we've been doing here with you. We're well on the way to completion here, and I think we can agree it's been pretty successful, so now's the time to think about how to roll it out to Don.

"I appreciate all the help you've been to us and know you're pleased with the work. So I'd like to ask if you could provide us with the intro to Don. He'll listen to you. Not a big deal, no presentation or anything, just a good word. All I really need is the intro; we'll take it from there. Let me know how you'd like to proceed."

Again, Amy is making withdrawals, not deposits, at the trust bank. Curt is being asked to give his good word to a colleague on behalf of someone else, in addition to presuming to judge his colleague's needs. There is considerable downside risk for Curt in this situation, and no apparent upside. He is likely to feel taken for granted. Let's analyze Amy's performance using the trust model.

Amy's trust score is higher than on Type 1, but still not near preexisting relationship levels. Both scores are much closer to what is expected in a completely new client scenario. Again, we must look at an additional relationship at stake: that between Curt (the original client) and Don (his colleague).

It is easy to assume that selling is all the responsibility of the professional firm advisors. In this version of cross-selling, however, there is a new client involved. In such a case, the existing client

Fig. 21.3. Trust Analysis of Amy, "I Just Need an Intro" Scenario

Trust Component	Comment
Credibility: 6	High on service offering, but low on Don's business
Reliability: 4	Track record with Curt, but not with Don, and no plan to get one
Intimacy: 2	Amy is asking Curt to pass judgment on Don's business needs and on Amy's quality; Amy takes no risk herself, Curt takes it all
Self-orientation: 8	All about Amy and her firm; no evidence of attention paid to what Don's interests are
Total Trust Score **1.5**	(C + R + I) / S = Trust (6 + 4 + 2) / 8 = 1.50

must be on the selling team. Why? Because the first client is apparently the most objective and the most likely to have interests in alignment with the potential client. There is every reason to include him, and no good way to exclude him. His absence from the sale would send negative signals.

How, then, do we get our clients to sell, much less manage them in so doing? The truth is, it need not be hard. What is required is to share an honest view of how the parties' interests are mutually intertwined.

To get one client to agree to actively sell to another client within the same organization, certain issues must be addressed. Foremost among those is the "what's in it for me?" question.

The content answers are not difficult. It may be in Curt's interest to help sell to Don for any of the following:

- The professional firm's prior client knowledge adds greatly to their content ability as a way to succeed.
- A good performance for Don will reflect well on Curt.
- Issues with Don that involve Curt will be handled from a perspective of knowledge and prior relationship.
- There may be scale economies of work between Curt and Don.
- Joint work offers political opportunities to improve relationships, enhance visibility, engender common points of view.
- Work done for Don may offer insights into work done for Curt.

These are rational reasons to convince the client helping with the selling, potentially very good reasons. Yet whether they are believed depends less on the content and more on the manner in which they are raised.

The words are in fact far less important than the belief behind them. The advisor must believe that the proposed cross-sell is in the best interest of the client organization. The advisor must believe that *not* to try to help on the client's additional problems would be unprofessional. Finally, the advisor must recognize that the help of the existing client is necessary to ensure that the client organization gains in the significant benefits at stake.

If it isn't true, the advisor shouldn't be saying it. If the advisor doesn't believe it, why should the client? But if he or she does believe it, the words will come. The lesson is to focus honestly on client benefits, and not to fear speaking the truth. If spoken to in this way, clients will sell to other clients, or will offer a good explanation for why they don't believe the value proposition in the first place.

Type 3 (Diversify)

Finally, we examine the situation where Amy wants to pitch a new service offering to Don, the new client executive. What is everyone thinking?

AMY: I know we could help out Don with our new service expertise, if Curt will just introduce Don and Barbara.

BARBARA: This could be a wild-goose chase. Amy doesn't know the buyer. Why should I follow her leads if they are no more likely to work out than my own?

CURT: I'm not sure I want to get caught between Amy and Don, much less with this Barbara involved.

DON: Curt wants me to meet with someone he doesn't know? Get real!

You can develop your own calculations for the trust equation in this scenario. It's clearly going to be much lower than the previous two!

If the sale is made, the relationship will be between Barbara and Don.

But think of all the other relationships at work here, including:

1. Amy and Curt
2. Amy and Barbara
3. Curt and Barbara
4. Curt and Don

Two crucial issues arise from this complexity: the sequencing of this sale, and dealing with its confusing emotional component.

Is there a right sequencing of this movement? Yes. It happens iteratively, and the internal sales come first. It may take one iteration or several.

If you are in this situation (as Amy), start by talking to your internal expert, Barbara. Then get more information from your client, having the courage to define the problem as you go along. Iterate again.

The right number of iterations is a matter of judgment; a rule of thumb might be when you can no longer think of a good reason *not* to proceed to a full, three- or four- person meeting.

Handled this way, the "real" meeting (the one involving all parties) will be a breeze if, and only if, all of the following is evident to everyone:

- That all parties invested serious time
- That the problem is well understood
- That the expertise is real and known
- That everyone's interest is genuine
- That everyone knows everyone

At this point, the initial promise of cross-selling can finally be delivered.

A Final (Hidden) Relationship

We must not forget that amid all this cross-selling activity, there is one more relationship that is going to be significantly affected no matter what happens: the relationship between Amy and Curt, the original two individuals involved.

Think about the many things the original advisor (Amy) is asking the client (Curt) to believe:

- That Barbara is an expert
- That Amy knows enough about the new service to know Barbara is an expert in it
- That Amy knows enough about Curt's business to know that the new service addresses a valid issue
- That Amy knows enough about Don's business to know that the new service addresses a valid issue
- That Amy has Curt's interests at heart as well as her own
- That Amy knows her firm's offering is competitive
- That the personal components of the existing relationship are not negated by the suggestion of a new business relationship

That is a lot to ask anyone to accept. It recasts the original relationship considerably. We repeat the key point of this chapter. It *can* be made to happen, but only where trust-building skills are well developed.

The usual tendency for people in Amy's position is to focus on creating credibility for the new-content expert, or for related business knowledge. But the bigger issues focus around Amy's personal credibility, and around the levels of intimacy and self-orientation that she exhibits.

Amy cannot rely on purely subjective assurances ("Barbara's really great; I've known her for a long time"). Those only draw down on trust. This is an issue of Amy's credibility, not of Barbara's.

Similarly, we (as Amy) often fall into the trap of thinking that either we must be as good a content expert as Barbara, or we have no right to say anything. The fact is, the client doesn't expect Amy to become an expert in the new content area. But the client *does* expect that Amy will learn enough about the business issue to be able to state that it is worth the client's time to talk to an expert. Again, the bigger issue is not the new expert's trust level, but the original advisor's trust level.

Our use of these scenarios may seem simplistic, but judge for yourself how common they are. The issue in cross-selling is not information quality and access; it is the creation of trust in fragile new relationships, where expectations are high and the hurdles great.

Handling the Tricky Emotions in Cross-Selling

Recall that the emotional trickiness of cross-selling arises from the fact that an institutional relationship can be helpful, but it cannot be tapped until the personal relationships are established or renegotiated, and those must be done as if they were brand new.

The key is to acknowledge (openly and candidly) the unspoken issues in each case. This is familiar to us; it is the key skill of naming and claiming. What is needed here is some version of this skill.

For example:

- "I don't know about you, but if I were in your shoes, I'd worry about bringing in someone new."

- "I can only presume that, since you know me from past work, you wouldn't tend to view me as an expert in this new field."

- "I know it's important to you to play a major role with your next client, so let me explain how that might work here."

- "Of course, I'll need to be very clear here because of the potential for appearing conflicted in suggesting you see Barbara."

- "I never take a recommendation blindly even from those I know and trust, so I don't expect you to either."

Issues that need to be raised explicitly are those that relate directly to the trust equation: credibility, reliability, the level and shared nature of intimacy, and the perception of self-orientation on the part of the advisor. The trust equation makes a good checklist for the professional seeking to ensure he or she has covered the bases.

Finally, we should note the symbolic importance of advisors investing their own time in the relationship as a *precursor* to the cross-selling sales activity. There is no better indication of our intentions than to spend our valuable time on someone. It proves that we are serious about our commitment to a shared agenda, that our orientation is not only to ourselves, and that we are committed to understanding the other's perspective.

It is through such signs that we communicate our willingness to engage in trust-based relationships.

22

The Quick-Impact List to Gain Trust

WHAT ARE THE TOP HIGHEST IMPACT or fastest payback things that people can do to gain trust? We are asked this question regularly. And it is valid.

So, here goes!

1. Listen to everything

Force yourself to listen and paraphrase. Get what they're trying to say. If you can't say it back in a way that has the speaker replying, "Yes, that's it, that's exactly what I'm saying," you haven't listened.

2. Empathize (for real)

Listening and paraphrasing let the other person know that he or she has been heard. But has he or she been understood? There's that nagging doubt until some form of empathetic statement is heard. You don't have to agree with what the other person says; you simply have to understand it.

Whenever you find yourself thinking, "This guy's an idiot," immediately ask yourself, "Why does he believe this? Where's he coming from? What happened to cause him to think this way?" You have to work *hard* at understanding other people. You must:

- Listen to where they're coming from
- Understand where they're coming from
- Acknowledge that you understand where they're coming from

Anyone who understands us has earned the right to engage in discussion and to be heard in return, even to argue with us. Anyone who empathizes with us has earned the right to disagree with us and still have our respect. They have greatly increased the odds of changing our mind.

3. Note what they're feeling

A purely emotional skill, this takes but a moment, but the payback is instant. Its only drawback is it feels risky. But its risk is far less than we think.

Salacuse says that to be a good advisor we have to pay attention to three things in every conversation: our client's words and actions (we would include feelings), our own words and actions (and feelings), *and* our client's *reaction* to our words and actions.

This can feel complex, but it can be easy. All it takes is a valid observation and a few words spoken from the heart. Examples: "You really look excited today! What's going on?" Or, leaning forward, "Joe, you seem distracted; something happening?"

The most powerful versions of this come from acknowledging a feeling about the other person, as well as our own feelings, if it is done with care. The same is true, though slightly less so, for observing feelings in third parties (e.g., "Joe seems a little listless lately; did his review upset him?").

4. Build that shared agenda

We can think of nothing easier than to practice the technique of a shared agenda. It may not yield the highest payoff but it is the easiest thing to do. Whether you're in a formal or informal meeting, on the phone, or in a large or small group, always start by sharing your idea of an agenda for the meeting and openly (and sincerely) asking the client to add his or her ideas to the agenda. It gives you immediate data, it models for the client the truth of your "we-not-me" attitude, and it creates buy-in.

5. Take a point of view, for goodness' sake!

It feels very risky to go out on a limb with an idea or perspective when you are not entirely sure of it because it involves personal risk. The truth is, it is extremely useful to our clients for us to be able to articulate a point of view, even if it ends up being rejected, or even wrong! There are two reasons: It stimulates reactions, and it crystallizes issues. Stating a point of view serves as a catalyst, a way of helping the client think.

Learn to express a point of view with a simple, emotional framing phrase such as: "Now let me just float a trial balloon here" or "This is probably not where we'll end up, but . . ." or "Hey, who knows where this might go, but it occurs to me that . . ."

6. Take a personal risk

Personal risk is when we feel we are putting a piece of ourselves "out there," revealing something about ourselves, becoming to some extent emotionally naked. We fear being ridiculed, or failing, or losing respect, or any of a thousand forms of emotional loss. Intimacy is the act of risking that personal loss. It doesn't have to be private. It just has to be personal. To risk something personal is to say that we are willing to increase the level of intimacy. It may or may not be reciprocated, but it's worth the attempt.

7. Ask about a related area

Most professions specialize and tend to focus on the issues and information relevant to the assignment at hand. But by doing so, they are potentially failing in their professional obligation to the client to notice and point out opportunities for improvement. Advisors who are willing to notice things outside their particular realm of expertise (and to naturally express that interest) make an impression on the client. The impression is that such advisors care, because, in fact, they do.

If your curiosity about the client's business has increased dramatically, this is a good sign; it means you care. You can be sure that articulating your questions to the client will be perceived as such.

8. Ask great questions

Open-ended questions force you to not prejudge what you are hearing, either by biasing the speaker, or by enforcing artificial categories. The objective is to hear what the speaker has to say in the speaker's own terms.

The emotional subtext of open-ended questions is one of respect; the listener pays the speaker the respect of allowing the speaker to set the frames of reference: his (or her) worldview, the sense of what is important and what isn't, what came first and what comes later, what is cause and what is effect.

9. Give away ideas

David Nadler, CEO of Delta Consulting, is a fan of this technique:

> "I'm not just a reflective psychotherapist who keeps saying, 'I understand, that must be tough.' That's a useful technique, but you've got to marry it to solutions. An idea that I got from one of our people is the technique of responding with three to five ideas—kind of idea generating. With an intro like 'These ideas might be wild and off the mark, but let's think about . . .'"

The conclusions many advisors draw are that they must be careful about giving away the store. First, they feel that the store is limited in nature. Second, it would hardly do to have the client discover that there is a limit to the store. Worst of all, it would be disastrous to have the client discover not only that the store is limited but that we have mastered only a part of it!

The truth is, expertise is like love: not only is it unlimited, you destroy it only by not giving it away. Love for a child is not cut in half with the birth of a second child. And expertise is not to be confused with what can be scanned into a database. The human capacity for problem redefinition and creativity is what a successful advisor brings to every situation. It is unlimited; it only gets better with practice.

10. Return calls unbelievably fast

Stephanie Wethered, the pastor referred to earlier, does this. She tries to return calls within ten minutes. She says it's the most trust-creating thing she does; no one expects it, and it demonstrates how much she values the other person.

11. Relax your mind

Here is a simple exercise for calming the stress before entering a stress-inducing environment such as a critical meeting. The purpose of this exercise is to temporarily cleanse your mind of internal distraction by spending some time concentrating your attention purely on a piece of wisdom.

"Some time" might mean sixty seconds at bedtime. It might mean several minutes in front of a keyboard or with a pencil, writing about what the wisdom means. Or it might mean talking out loud to oneself in the car for a few minutes before the client phone call or meeting.

Here is a list of such "sayings" built around key precepts of this book. Think about only one at a time. The others will wait for another day.

1. It's about the client.
2. Who am I thinking about?
3. What is the client feeling about this?
4. The answer is a better question.
5. The problem is rarely what the client said it was at first.
6. I am not the center of the universe.
7. Who am I serving by my present approach?
8. Assigning blame will trap me; taking responsibility will empower me.
9. It's a "we" game, not a "me" game.
10. What am I afraid of here?
11. Knowing the truth is better than not knowing it.
12. You can hope for what might be, but don't wish for what can't be.
13. A point of view doesn't commit you for life.
14. Don't ever, ever tell a lie or even shade the truth.

More Tips

1. Notice a feeling in yourself and comment on it.
2. Make a commitment and then deliver on it—not overdeliver or underdeliver, just deliver.
3. Don't answer a question the first time the client asks it; ask for clarification.
4. Say something revealing about yourself, but not manipulatively.
5. Make a facial expression of empathy, even if it's just scrunching up your face and saying "ouch" in an appropriate setting.
6. Reach out to notice, and acknowledge, something that has been held back in or about the other person.

Top Things to Remind Yourself

1. I don't have to prove myself every ten seconds.
2. I have a right to be here in this room; I can add value without worrying about it.
3. Shut up and repeat again and again: "Really? And then what happened?"
4. Also again and again: "Gee, what's behind that?"
5. Is my pulse racing? Why? Why not say so, and say why, out loud?
6. Have I earned the right yet to give an answer?
7. Am I trying in any way to win an argument? Turn it back into a conversation.
8. Emulate Lt. Columbo: "I may be a little slow here. Maybe it's just me, but . . ."
9. Take responsibility for the emotional outcome.
10. Don't blame anybody for anything anytime.
11. More value is added through problem definition than through problem answer.
12. Just because the client asks a question doesn't mean that's the right question to answer.
13. Don't be insecure. Say to yourself: "Hey, if I don't know the answer, and I'm a pro, then this is a really neat question; lets get into it!"
14. Is my tummy telling me something's wrong? My tummy's right. Let's talk about it.

Two Final Suggestions

1. Call your client, now!
2. Tell your romantic partner how much he or she is appreciated. Do it today!

APPENDIX:
A COMPILATION OF OUR LISTS

This appendix duplicates all of the lists we present in the book. You can use them in any of three ways:

- Skim them all to get a feel for the contents of the book.
- Use them to identify a topic of interest and go straight to that chapter.
- Use them as reminders after you have read the book (and add to them as you accumulate experiences).

The More Your Clients Trust You, the More They Will
(Chapter 1)

1. Reach for your advice
2. Be inclined to accept and act on your recommendations
3. Bring you in on more advanced, complex, strategic issues
4. Treat you as you wish to be treated
5. Respect you
6. Share more information that helps you to help them, and improves the quality of the service you provide
7. Pay your bills without question
8. Refer you to their friends and business acquaintances
9. Lower the level of stress in your interactions
10. Give you the benefit of the doubt
11. Forgive you when you make a mistake
12. Protect you when you need it (even from their own organization)
13. Warn you of dangers that you might avoid
14. Be comfortable and allow you to be comfortable
15. Involve you early on when their issues begin to form, rather than later in the process (or maybe even call you first!)
16. Trust your instincts and judgments (including those about other people such as your colleagues and theirs)

Common Traits of Trusted Advisors

(Chapter 1)

1. Seem to understand us, effortlessly, and like us
2. Are consistent (we can depend on them)
3. Always help us see things from fresh perspectives
4. Don't try to force things on us
5. Help us think things through (it's our decision)
6. Don't substitute their judgment for ours
7. Don't panic or get overemotional (they stay calm)
8. Help us *think* and separate our logic from our emotion
9. Criticize and correct us gently, lovingly
10. Don't pull their punches (we can rely on them to tell us the truth)
11. Are in it for the long haul (the relationship is more important than the current issue)
12. Give us reasoning (to help us think), not just their conclusions
13. Give us options, increase our understanding of those options, give us their recommendation, and let us choose
14. Challenge our assumptions (help us uncover the false assumptions we've been working under)
15. Make us feel comfortable and casual personally (but they take the issues seriously)
16. Act like a real person, not someone in a role
17. Are reliably on our side and always seem to have our interests at heart
18. Remember everything we ever said (without notes)
19. Are always honorable (they don't gossip about others, and we trust their values)
20. Help us put our issues in context, often through the use of metaphors, stories, and anecdotes (few problems are completely unique)
21. Have a sense of humor to diffuse (our) tension in tough situations
22. Are smart (sometimes in ways we're not)

Common Attributes of Trusted Advisors

(Chapter 2)

1. Have a predilection to focus on the client, rather than themselves. They have:
   - enough self-confidence to listen without prejudging
   - enough curiosity to inquire without supposing an answer
   - willingness to see the client as co-equal in a joint journey
   - enough ego strength to subordinate their own ego
2. Focus on the client as an individual, not as a person fulfilling a role
3. Believe that a continued focus on problem definition and resolution is as important as technical or content mastery
4. Show a strong "competitive" drive aimed not at competitors, but at constantly finding new ways to be of greater service to the client
5. Consistently focus on doing the next right thing, rather than on aiming for specific outcomes
6. Are motivated more by an internalized drive to do the right thing than by their own organization's rewards or dynamics
7. View methodologies, models, management techniques, and business processes as means to an end
8. Believe that success in client relationships is tied to the accumulation of quality experiences
9. Believe that both selling and serving are aspects of professionalism
10. Believe that there is a distinction between a business life and a private life, but that both lives are very personal (i.e., human)

Three Basic Skills a Trusted Advisor Needs

(Chapters 3–5)

1. Earning trust
2. Giving advice effectively
3. Building relationships

Some Characteristics of Trust Relationships

(Chapter 3)

1. Grows, rather than just appears
2. Is both rational and emotional
3. Presumes a two-way relationship
4. Is intrinsically about perceived risk
5. Is different for the client than it is for the advisor
6. Is personal

Principles of Relationship Building
(Chapter 5)

1. Go first
2. Illustrate, don't tell
3. Listen for what's different, not for what's familiar
4. Be sure your advice is being sought
5. Earn the right to offer advice
6. Keep asking
7. Say what you mean
8. When you need help, ask for it
9. Show an interest in the person
10. Use compliments, not flattery
11. Show appreciation

Important Mindsets
(Chapter 6)

1. Ability to focus on the other person
2. Self-confidence
3. Ego strength
4. Curiosity
5. Inclusive professionalism

Four Essential Elements That Engender Trust
(Chapter 8)

1. Credibility
2. Reliability
3. Intimacy
4. A low level of self-orientation, or focus on oneself

Some Tips on Enhancing Credibility

(Chapter 8)

1. Figure out how to tell as much truth as possible, except where doing so would injure others.

2. Don't tell lies, or even exaggerate. At all. Ever.

3. Avoid saying things that others might construe as lies.

4. Speak with expression, not monotonically. Use body language, eye contact, and vocal range. Show the client you have energy around the subject at hand.

5. Don't just cite references. Where it is genuinely possible to create mutual benefit, introduce your clients to each other; they will learn from each other, and you will have plenty of reflected credit in which to bask.

6. When you don't know, say so, quickly and directly.

7. Yes it's important to have them know your credentials. Just don't get silly by having all those initials and certifications appear after your name on your business card.

8. Relax. You know much more than you think you know. If you don't really belong there, then don't put yourself there in the first place.

9. Make sure you've done absolutely all your homework on the client company, the client marketplace, and the client individual, and that it's absolutely up to the minute.

10. There's no reason to show off.

11. Love your topic. It will show.

Some Thoughts on Reliability

(Chapter 8)

1. Make specific commitments to your client around small things: getting that article by tomorrow, placing the call, writing the draft by Monday, looking up a reference. And then deliver on them, quietly, and on time.

2. Send meeting materials in advance so that the client has the option of reviewing them in advance, saving meeting time for substantive discussions.

3. Make sure meetings have clear goals, not just agendas, and ensure the goals are met.

4. Use the client's "fit and feel" around terminology, style, formats, hours.

5. Review agendas with your client, before meetings, before phone calls, before discussions. Clients should know that they can expect you to always solicit their views on how time will be spent.

6. Reconfirm scheduled events before they happen. Announce changes to scheduled or committed dates *as soon as* they change.

Some Thoughts on Intimacy

(Chapter 8)

1. Be not afraid! Creating intimacy requires courage, not just for you, but for everyone.

2. People in senior positions appreciate candor, but candor isn't necessarily intimacy, and they value that even more.

3. Find the fun and fascination.

4. Test whether you're coming too close to the line, or pushing too far, too fast.

5. Practice a little. No, you can't practice spontaneity, but you can practice phrasing.

"Threats" to Client Focus

(Chapter 8)

1. Selfishness
2. Self-consciousness
3. A need to appear on top of things
4. A desire to look intelligent
5. A to-do list on our mind that is a mile long
6. A desire to jump to the solution
7. A desire to win that exceeds the desire to help the client
8. A desire to be right
9. A desire to be seen to be right
10. A desire to be seen as adding value
11. Fears of various kinds: fear of not knowing, of not having the right answer, of not appearing intelligent, of being rejected

Clues About Excessive Self-Orientation

(Chapter 8)

1. A tendency to relate their stories to ourselves
2. A need to too quickly finish their sentences for them
3. A need to fill empty spaces in conversations
4. A need to appear clever, bright, witty, etc.
5. An inability to provide a direct answer to a direct question
6. An unwillingness to say we don't know
7. Name-dropping of other clients
8. A recitation of qualifications
9. A tendency to give answers too quickly
10. A tendency to want to have the last word
11. Closed ended questions early on
12. Putting forth hypotheses or problem statements before fully hearing the client's hypotheses or problem statements
13. Passive listening; a lack of visual and verbal cues that indicate the client is being heard
14. Watching the client as if he/she were a television set (merely a source of data)

Signs of Low Self-Orientation

(Chapter 8)

1. Letting the client fill in the empty spaces
2. Asking the client to talk about what's behind an issue
3. Using open-ended questions
4. Not giving answers until the right is earned to do so (and the client will let you know when you have earned it)
5. Focusing on defining the problem, not guessing the solution
6. Reflective listening, summarizing what we've heard to make sure we heard correctly what was said and what was intended
7. Saying you don't know when you don't know
8. Acknowledging the feelings of the client (with respect)
9. Learning to tell the client's story before we write our own
10. Listening to clients without distractions: door closed, phone off, email not in line of sight, frequent eye contact
11. Resisting with confidence a client's invitation to provide a solution too early on—to stay in the listening and joint problem definition phases of discussion
12. Trusting in our ability to add value *after* listening, rather than trying to do so *during* listening
13. Taking most of the responsibility for failed communications

The Five-Step Trust-Building Process

(Chapter 9)

1. Engage: Uses language of interest and concern
2. Listen: Uses language of understanding and empathy
3. Frame: Uses language of perspective and candor
4. Envision: Uses language of possibility
5. Commit: Uses language of joint exploration

Skills Required for the Five-Step Trust Process

(Chapter 9)

1. Engaging requires the skill of being (credibly) noticed.
2. Listening requires an ability to *understand* another human being.
3. Framing requires creative insight and emotional courage.
4. Envisioning requires a spirit of collaboration and creativity.
5. Commitment requires the ability to generate enthusiasm, and sometimes the ability to manage down overenthusiasm.

Approaches to Engagement

(Chapter 10)

1. Approaches that demonstrate concern about competitive developments
2. Approaches that signal an understanding of career challenges facing a particular individual
3. Approaches that might offer a solution to a specific managerial issue
4. Approaches that demonstrate continuity and development

What Good Listeners Do

(Chapter 11)

1. Probe for clarification
2. Listen for unvoiced emotions
3. Listen for the story
4. Summarize well
5. Empathize
6. Listen for what's different, not for what's familiar
7. Take it all seriously (they don't say, "You shouldn't worry about that")
8. Spot hidden assumptions
9. Let the client "get it out of his or her system"
10. Ask "How do you feel about that?"
11. Keep the client talking ("What else have you considered?")
12. Keep asking for more detail that helps them understand
13. Get rid of distractions while listening
14. Focus on hearing your version first
15. Let you tell your story your way
16. Stand in your shoes, at least while they're listening
17. Ask you how you think they might be of help
18. Ask what you've thought of before telling you what they've thought of
19. Look at (not stare at) the client as he or she speaks
20. Look for congruity (or incongruity) between what the client says and how he or she gestures and postures
21. Make it seem as if the client is the only thing that matters and that they have all the time in the world.
22. Encourage by nodding head or giving a slight smile
23. Are aware of and control their body movement (no moving around, shaking legs, fiddling with a paper clip)

What Great Listeners Don't Do

(Chapter 11)

1. Interrupt
2. Respond too soon
3. Match the client's points ("Oh, yes, I had something like that happen to me. It all started . . .")
4. Editorialize in midstream ("Well, that option's a nonstarter")
5. Jump to conclusions (much less judgments)
6. Ask closed-end questions for no reason
7. Give you their ideas before hearing yours
8. Judge you
9. Try to solve the problem too quickly
10. Take calls or interruptions in the course of a client meeting. (It seems so obvious, but watch how often it happens!)

Characteristics of Naming and Claiming

(Chapter 12)

1. An acknowledgment of the difficulty of raising the issue
2. An acceptance of the responsibility for raising it
3. A direct statement of the issue itself

Responsibility-Taking Caveats

(Chapter 12)

1. It's probably just me, but . . .
2. I must have been tuned out for a moment, I'm sorry, but . . .
3. I'm sure you covered this before, but . . .
4. I'm sorry to interrupt but I just can't get this out of my head about . . .
5. You've probably thought of this already, but . . .
6. I wish I knew, but I just don't know how to handle this concern . . .
7. I realize you have a strong preference for XYZ, but . . .
8. I'm probably thinking about this all wrong, but . . .
9. I'm not sure if this is on-point, but . . .
10. I may not have understood this right, but . . .
11. I don't know exactly how to say this, so I hope you'll help me, but . . .
12. I'm not sure if I'm being inappropriate in bringing this up, but . . .
13. I hope you'll forgive me for not knowing quite how to say this, but . . .

Commitment Topics

(Chapter 14)

1. What's going to get in the way of getting this done?
2. What do we intend to do about it?
3. Who needs to be brought into the loop?
4. Who should do what part?
5. What information do we need?
6. When shall we check in?
7. What are the key deadlines?

Managing Expectations

(Chapter 14)

1. Clearly articulate what we will do and won't do
2. Clearly articulate what the client will do and won't do
3. Define the boundaries of the analyses we will perform
4. Check with the client about areas that the client may not want us to get involved in, or any people the client does not want us to speak with
5. Identify precise working arrangements
6. Agree on methods and frequency of communicating
7. Decide who should get which reports
8. Decide how often a report should be delivered
9. Decide how any reports will get used
10. Decide what milestones and progress reviews are needed
11. Decide how success will be measured, both at the end and during the process

Building Trust When Managing Expectations

(Chapter 14)

1. Always tell the truth about what you can (and can't) do, and what you can (and can't) deliver when.
2. Start the project before you've been engaged.
3. Show your enthusiasm.
4. Ask the questions that are troubling you earlier rather than later.

Concerns About the Trust-Based Approach

(Chapter 15)

1. This is all too personally risky. The emotional stuff feels embarrassing, different, flaky.

2. It's not easy to stop worrying about yourself and focus on others instead.

3. Professional services firms often breed a culture of content expertise and mastery. (We're taught that content is all.)

4. We can't overcome our fears of looking ignorant, stupid, or uninformed, so we act assertively.

5. It's hard to shut up and listen before you solve the problem. We have a hard time rewiring our instincts or habits.

6. It takes a lot of courage to speak about the unspeakable. Some things you just don't say; they're too personal, too risky, or too unprofessional.

7. It comes too close to the line of invading the private.

8. This approach discounts too heavily the value of good content or expertise.

9. It all sounds too moralistic.

10. This process sounds s-l-o-w! My budget won't allow for this!

11. My client wants me to focus on the work at hand; he or she doesn't want to see me about anything else.

12. It's risky to take a position on an issue until I'm absolutely sure.

13. I took a position, and now I'm stuck with it. To change my view would destroy my credibility!

14. It's hard to be this humble!

Why Professionals Jump to Action Too Soon

(Chapter 15)

1. The human tendency to focus on ourselves

2. The belief that we're selling only content

3. The desire for tangibility

4. The search for validation

Common Fears

(Chapter 15)

1. Not having the answer
2. Not being able to get the right answer quickly
3. Having the wrong answer
4. Committing some social faux pas
5. Looking confused
6. Not knowing how to respond
7. Having missed some information
8. Revealing some ignorance
9. Misdiagnosing

Other Emotions One Must Control

(Chapter 15)

1. Wanting (needing?) to take credit for an idea
2. Wanting to fill blank airtime with content
3. Playing to our own insecurity by feeling we have to get all our credentials out there
4. Wanting to put a cap on the problem so we can solve it later, without the pressure
5. Wanting to hedge our answers in case we're wrong
6. Wanting (too soon) to relate our own version of the client's story or problem

Dealing with Different Client Types

(Chapter 16)

1. Work in advance on what is different about this client, and what might be different about you in this situation.

   - Are there any topics I should avoid because they are too delicate to discuss in a large forum?

   - Are there any topics on which the views of your colleagues are divided?

   - Where are we likely to encounter the most resistance?

   - Do you have initiatives already going on that might interact with the discussion of this one?

2. As you look at a client, force yourself to ask three questions:

   - What is the client's prevailing personal motivation?

   - What is their personality?

   - How does the state of their organization affect their worldview?

3. When thinking about a client's prevailing personal motivation, which of the following comes first?

   - the need to excel?

   - the need to take action and achieve results?

   - the need to understand and analyze before deciding?

   - the need to drive consensus?

4. Figure out why you might truly like this client as a person.

5. Use the trust equation.

Some Difficult Client Types, and How to Respond

(Chapter 16)

Type 1. The "Just the Facts, Ma'am" Client

Type 2. The "I'll Get Back to You" Client

Type 3. The "You're the Expert, Dummy" Client

Type 4. The "Let Me Handle That" Client

Type 5. The "Let's Go Through This Again" Client

Type 6. The "You Don't Understand" Client

Type 7. The "My Enemy's Enemy Is My Friend" Client

Type 8. The "Just Like, You Know, Come On" Client

Type 9. The "Oh, By the Way" Client

Factors Affecting a Client's Perceived Value of Service (Chapter 19)

1. Understanding
2. Sense of control
3. Sense of progress
4. Access and availability
5. Responsiveness
6. Reliability
7. Appreciation
8. Sense of importance
9. Respect

Tactics to Build Trust on the Assignment

(Chapter 19)

1. Involving the client in the process through:
   - brainstorming sessions
   - giving the client tasks to perform
   - giving the client options and letting the client choose
   - keeping the client informed on what's going to happen, when, and why

2. Making reports and presentations more useful, easier to pass on, by:
   - getting the client to instruct us on format and presentation
   - providing a summary so the client can use it internally without modification
   - having all reports read by a non-project person to ensure readability and comprehension prior to delivery
   - providing all charts, tables, and summaries on overheads for internal client use

3. Helping the client use what we deliver by:
   - coaching the client in dealing with others in client organization
   - empowering the client with reasoning steps
   - advising on tactics/politics of how results should be shared inside client organization
   - writing progress summaries in a way that the client can use internally without modification

4. Making meetings more valuable by:
   - establishing a specific agenda and goals prior to meeting
   - sending information and reports in advance, saving meeting time for discussion, not presentation
   - finding out attendees in advance and researching them
   - establishing next steps for both sides
   - dictating and transcribing a summary of all meetings and significant phone conversations and sending copy to client the same day or next day
   - Calling afterward to confirm that goals were met

5. Being accessible and available by:
   - calling in advance when we're going to be unavailable
   - ensuring that our assistants know where we are and when we'll be back
   - ensuring that our assistants know the names of all clients and names of all team members involved in the relationship
   - working at getting clients comfortable with our "junior" personnel, so they can be available when we're not

Building Trust During the Engagement Process

(Chapter 19)

1. Keep clients in the loop regarding your progress.
2. Tell the truth and not what the client wants to hear.
3. Love your work.
4. Make sure that your answer is not a purely technical one.
5. Figure out what comes next for the client.
6. Don't ask for follow-on work too quickly.

Client Suggestions for Relationship Building

(Chapter 20)

1. Make an impact on our business, don't just be visible.
2. Do more things "on spec" (i.e., invest your time on preliminary work in new areas).
3. Spend more time helping us think, and helping us develop strategies.
4. Lead our thinking. Tell us what our business is going to look like five or ten years from now.
5. *Jump* on any new pieces of information we have, so you can stay up-to-date on what's going on in our business. Use our data to give us an extra level of analysis. Ask for it, don't wait for us to give it to you.
6. Schedule some offsite meetings together. Join us for brainstorming sessions about our business.
7. Make an extra effort to understand how our business works: sit in on our meetings.
8. Help us see how we compare to others, both within and outside our industry.
9. Tell me why our competitors are doing what they're doing.
10. Discuss with us other things we should be doing; we welcome any and all ideas!

The Quick-Impact List to Gain Trust
(Chapter 22)

1. Listen to everything
2. Empathize (for real)
3. Note what they're feeling
4. Build that shared agenda
5. Take a point of view, for goodness' sake!
6. Take a personal risk
7. Ask about a related area
8. Ask great questions
9. Give away ideas
10. Return calls unbelievably fast
11. Relax your mind

Sayings to Relax Your Mind
(Chapter 22)

1. It's about the client.
2. Who am I thinking about?
3. What is the client feeling about this?
4. The answer is a better question.
5. The problem is rarely what the client said it was at first.
6. I am not the center of the universe.
7. Who am I serving by my present approach?
8. Assigning blame will trap me; taking responsibility will empower me.
9. It's a "we" game, not a "me" game.
10. What am I afraid of here?
11. Knowing the truth is better than not knowing it.
12. You can hope for what might be, but don't wish for what can't be.
13. A point of view doesn't commit you for life.
14. Don't ever, ever tell a lie or even shade the truth.

More Tips

(Chapter 22)

1. Notice a feeling in yourself and comment on it.
2. Make a commitment and then deliver on it—not overdeliver or underdeliver, just deliver.
3. Don't answer a question the first time the client asks it; ask for clarification.
4. Say something revealing about yourself, but not manipulatively.
5. Make a facial expression of empathy, even if it's just scrunching up your face and saying "ouch" in an appropriate setting.
6. Reach out to notice, and acknowledge, something that has been held back in or about the other person.

Top Things to Remind Yourself

(Chapter 22)

1. I don't have to prove myself every ten seconds.
2. I have a right to be here in this room; I can add value without worrying about it.
3. Shut up and repeat again and again: "Really? And then what happened?"
4. Also again and again: "Gee, what's behind that?"
5. Is my pulse racing? Why? Why not say so, and say why, out loud?
6. Have I earned the right yet to give an answer?
7. Am I trying in any way to win an argument? Turn it back into a conversation.
8. Emulate Lt. Columbo: "I may be a little slow here. Maybe it's just me, but . . ."
9. Take responsibility for the emotional outcome.
10. Don't blame anybody for anything anytime.
11. More value is added through problem definition than through problem answer.
12. Just because the client asks a question doesn't mean that's the right question to answer.
13. Don't be insecure. Say to yourself: "Hey, if I don't know the answer, and I'm a pro, then this is a really neat question; lets get into it!"
14. Is my tummy telling me something's wrong? My tummy's right. Let's talk about it.

Two Final Suggestions

(Chapter 22)

1. Call your client, now!
2. Tell your romantic partner how much he or she is appreciated. Do it today!

ACKNOWLEDGMENTS

We must first thank our families for their support, and for the lessons they have taught us about the importance of trusting relationships (and the benefits of getting good advice!).

We are also grateful to the many consulting clients and participants in workshops, seminars, and training programs who bore with us as we tried to articulate and communicate our ideas.

Many people have helped directly with the manuscript of this book as it developed through numerous drafts. All three of us have benefited from insights contributed by our spouses, and our thanks for substantive contributions go to Kathy, Renée, and Susan.

David's assistant and business manager, Julie MacDonald O'Leary, was the only person other than the authors to read and critique every draft. She provided invaluable input (as always) at every stage. Of the many readers of the manuscript, Patrick McKenna and Gerald Riskin of The Edge Group (collaborators with David on the PracticeCoach© program) were particularly generous with their time and ideas. We appreciate the opportunity to "borrow" their best ones.

Our thanks also go to John Butman, who was extremely helpful to Charlie and Rob in structuring and organizing their ideas, contributing to their thinking, and thoughtful about how to describe the difficult topic of trust, among other contributions.

John Barch deserves special thanks for his early encouragement to Charlie and Rob.

In addition to those mentioned, the following practicing trusted advisors were kind enough to read the manuscript and contribute ideas:

Fiona Czerniawska, Tom Colleton, David Gaylin, Candace Harris, Marco Materazzi, Jon Moynihan, Scott Parker, Frances Sacker, Chris Starrett, and Robbie Vorhaus.

Finally, we would like to acknowledge the individuals who

were kind enough to grant us interviews and share their experience with us, including: Peter Biagetti, George Colony, Jim Copeland, Jim Kelly, Richard Mahoney, David Nadler, Regina M. Pisa, Alan Schwartz, Joe Sherman, Stephanie Weathered, Tim White, and the management teams at Digitas, Inc., and Forrester Research.

NOTES AND REFERENCES

Chapter 2: What Is a Trusted Advisor?

The "levels of a business relationship" diagrams were inspired, in part, by Robert B. Miller and Stephen E. Heiman with Tad Tuleja, *Successful Large Account Management*, Henry Holt, 1991, p. 56.

Robert Falk and Michael Jordan story: Henry Louis Gates, Jr. "Net Worth," *The New Yorker*, June 1, 1998, p. 48.

Buffett-Munger story: Transcript of panel session between Warren Buffett and Bill Gates, *Fortune*, July 20, 1998.

Mahoney-Shutack quote: Interview with Rob Galford, 1999.

James Kelly quote: Interview with Charlie Green, 1999.

Regina M. Pisa: Interview with Rob Galford, 1999.

Study of students and faculty: "Divergent Realities and Convergent Disappointments in the Hierarchic Relation: Trust and the Intuitive Auditor at Work," by Roderick M. Kramer, in *Trust in Organizations: Frontiers of Theory and Research*, edited by Roderick M. Kramer and Tom R. Tyler, Sage Publications, 1996.

Chapter 3: Earning Trust

Peter Biagetti story: Interview with Rob Galford, 1999.

Alan Schwartz anecdote: Interview with David Maister, 2000.

Chapter 4: How to Give Advice

The concept of the emotional duet is from Jeswald W. Salacuse, *The Art of Advice*, Times Books, 1994.

Chapter 5: The Rules of Romance

Robert Cialdini, *Influence*, Quill, 1989.

Chapter 6: The Importance of Mindsets

Dale Carnegie, *How to Win Friends and Influence People*, Pocket Books, 1982, p. 33

Tim White story: Observed by Charlie Green, 1998.

David Nadler quote: Interview with Charlie Green, 1999.

For more on the distinction between being a technician and being a professional, see David H. Maister, *True Professionalism*, Free Press, 1997.

Stephanie Weathered quote: Interview with Charlie Green, 1999.

Joe Sherman quote: Interview with Rob Galford, 1999.

Chapter 7: Sincerity or Technique?

Gerald M. Weinberg, *The Secrets of Consulting*, Dorset House, 1985.

Liking or tolerating clients: David H. Maister, *True Professionalism*, Free Press, 1997, chap. 2.

Chapter 8: The Trust Equation

Pioneering work on formulating equations for trust was done over twenty years ago by the consulting firm Synectics, Cambridge, Mass. However, the formulation shown here is our own.

For a discussion of the economics of new and existing clients, see Frederick F. Reichheld, *The Loyalty Effect*, HBS Publishing, 1996.

Chapter 10: Engagement

William Brooks and Thomas M. Travesano, *You're Working Too Hard to Make the Sale*, Richard D. Irwin, 1995.

Steven Covey, A. Roger Merrill, and Rebecca R. Merrill, *First Things First*, Simon & Schuster, 1994.

Chapter 11: The Art of Listening

Jack Welch quote: "Master of the M&A Universe," *Business Week*, March, 1997.

Jim Copeland quote: Interview with Rob Galford and Charlie Green, 1999.

Tony Alessandra, *The Dynamics of Effective Listening*, (audiotape) Nightingale Conant, no date.

Chapter 14: Commitment

The discussion on managing expectations is based, in part, on Peter Block, *Flawless Consulting*, Jossey-Bass, 2nd Edition, 1999.

Chapter 15: What's So Hard About All This?

New York Times survey: Andrew J. Cherlin, "I'm OK, You're Selfish," *New York Times*, Sunday Magazine, October 17, 1999.

Chapter 16: Differing Client Types

Clients' primary personal motivation: LIFO and Life Orientations Training, Dr. Stuart Atkins, Stuart Atkins, Inc., Beverly Hills, Calif.

Chapter 19: Building Trust on the Current Assignment

David H. Maister, *Managing the Professional Service Firm*, Free Press, 1993.

Chapter 22: The Quick-Impact List

David Nadler quote: Interview with Charlie Green, 1999.

Stephanie Weathered: Interview with Charlie Green, 1999.

INDEX

ABOUT THE AUTHORS

David H. Maister is widely acknowledged as the world's leading authority on the management of professional service firms. For nearly two decades he has advised firms in a broad spectrum of professions, covering all strategic and managerial issues.

David has a global practice, spending about 40 percent of his time in North America, 30 percent in Western Europe, and 30 percent in the rest of the world.

A native of Great Britain, David holds degrees from the University of Birmingham, the London School of Economics, and the Harvard Business School, where he was a professor for seven years.

He is the author of the best-selling books *Managing the Professional Service Firm* (1993) and *True Professionalism* (1997), which are his eighth and ninth books. Many of his articles have been translated into the major European languages (including Russian), and his books are available in Dutch, Spanish, Indonesian, Korean, Polish, Serbo-Croatian, and Chinese (Mandarin.)

He lives in Boston, Massachusetts. He may be reached at:
Tel: 617-262-5968
E-mail: David_Maister@msn.com
Web site: www.davidmaister.com

Charles H. Green is an executive educator and business strategy consultant to the professional services industry. Charlie has taught in executive education programs for the Kellogg Graduate School of Management at Northwestern University, and for Columbia University Graduate School of Business, as well as independently through his firm, Trusted Advisor Associates. His current work centers on the nature of trust-based relationships within organizations, and on the management of professional service firms.

Charlie is a graduate of Columbia and of the Harvard Business School. He spent the first twenty years of his career with The MAC Group and its successor, Gemini Consulting, where his roles included strategy consulting (in Europe and the United States), VP Strategic

Planning, and a variety of other firm leadership roles. He is the author of numerous papers, with articles published in the *Harvard Business Review* and *Management Horizons*. He founded Trusted Advisor Associates with Rob Galford. He resides in Morristown, New Jersey. He may be reached at:

Tel: 973-898-1579

E-mail: cgreen@trustedadvisor.com

Web site: www.trustedadvisor.com

Robert M. Galford is currently the executive vice president and chief people officer of Digitas, Inc., a leading Internet professional services firm with over 1,400 employees. He taught for many years on executive programs at the Columbia Graduate School of Business and the Kellogg Graduate School of Management at Northwestern University, in addition to consulting to professional services firms, technology companies, and financial institutions.

Rob has lived and worked in both Western Europe and North America as a vice president of The MAC Group and its successor firm, Gemini Consulting. He has practiced law with the international firm of Curtis, Mallet-Prevost, Colt & Mosle in New York and Washington, and has also worked in investment management for Citicorp.

Rob's writing and commentaries on management have been published in the *Boston Globe* and he is a three-time contributor to the *Harvard Business Review*. He currently sits on the boards of directors of Forrester Research, Inc., and Access Data Corporation. He also hosts the business video, *Talk About Change!* with the popular cartoon character Dilbert.

His educational background includes Liceo Segre, Turin, Italy; a B.A. in economics and Italian literature from Haverford College; an M.B.A. from Harvard, and a J.D. from Georgetown University Law Center, where he was an associate editor of *The Tax Lawyer*. Rob lives with his family in Concord, Massachusetts. He may be reached at:

E-mail: rgalford@tiac.net